Acknowledgements

Welcome to the fourth edition of *The Kinship Care Guide*
with kinship carers as we've updated this edition. They t...
found helpful as they started their kinship journey. In writing this updated e...
there are many people we would like to thank.

We would firstly like to thank all the kinship carers who kindly shared their insights and experiences with us. They've helped us to develop and review both new and existing information. Their insight has led us to add new chapters. It covers topics like education, working with your local authority and legal proceedings.

With thanks to:

- Ian Pearce, kinship carer and member of the Kinship Care Advisory Group
- Jan Clampett, kinship carer and member of the Kinship Care Advisory Group
- Jenny Wye, kinship carer and member of Kinship Care Advisory Group
- Kay Hall, kinship carer
- Keith Whittaker, kinship carer and member of the Kinship Care Advisory Group
- Kieron Town, kinship carer and Kinship volunteer
- Lorna Burke, kinship carer
- Michelle Hall, kinship carer and member of the Kinship Care Advisory Group
- Rob Lindsay, kinship carer
- Wendy Turner, kinship carer and member of the Kinship Care Advisory Group
- Zoe Patterson, kinship carer

Thanks also to those kinship carers who completed surveys and questionnaires, sharing their tips, knowledge, and expertise. You will find these scattered throughout this guide. Whether it's in checklists, quotes, or case studies.

We would also like to thank all of the experts who gave their input, advice and knowledge to review the content in this guide.

This includes:

- Helen Moody, Partner, Ridley and Hall Legal
- Khalida Haque, former Lead Therapeutic Practitioner, Kinship
- Dr Louise Sims, former Head of Research and Practice, Kinship
- Michelle Hall BA (hons), MA, PhD, AFHEA Leeds Trinity University
- Neil Barton, Education Consultant, Leeds Virtual School
- Nicola Kerr, Senior Advice Worker, Kinship
- Nigel Priestley MBE, Senior Partner, Ridley and Hall Legal
- Dr Paul McGrath, Social Worker, volunteer advisor to Kinship
- Sam Turner, Associate Director of Policy and Public Affairs, Kinship

Finally, we want to say thank you to the people who laid the foundations for this guide. In particular we would like to thank the authors of previous editions of the guide:

- Our friend Doug Lawson, an independent children's services consultant, who generously gave his time to support our work with kinship families
- Jo Raine, a former Advice Service Manager at Kinship

This guide is dedicated to kinship carers who have stepped up to care for more than 132,000 children in England. No matter where you are on your journey, know you're not alone.

Contents

Welcome

Well done. You've opened the first page. You may be feeling overwhelmed, tired, and unsupported. However, if you are a kinship carer, like me, I promise that within these pages you will find golden nuggets of information, wisdom, fresh understanding, hope, and encouragement for the future. No matter what stage of the journey you are on.

This guide has been written in partnership with kinship carers like me. For kinship carers like you. No matter what type of kinship arrangement you have. It is easy to follow, relevant for all, with case studies, links to detailed information and further support that will strengthen, empower, and equip you for the journey you are on.

My wife and I became special guardians 7 years ago. We had 15 minutes to decide whether we would take care of 2 little girls because our friends couldn't. Of course, the answer was "yes". From that moment, our search for good quality, unbiased, and consistent information started. Sadly, there was very little information available, and nothing we could find written in partnership with kinship carers.

We quickly realised that knowledge is power. It allows carers like us to speak with authority when working with professionals who are there to support us. Having not had this information at the early stages of our journey, I have worked tirelessly with Kinship to improve this Kinship Care Guide for England and other information that helps us care for the children we are responsible for.

If I'd had this guide at the beginning of our journey, we wouldn't have been so confused or stressed. We would have understood more about our rights, responsibilities, the support we could ask for and questions to ask.

Since becoming kinship carers, much has changed. The first National Kinship Care Strategy was published in December 2023 with a definition of what kinship care is. It explains the need for improvements to kinship care. In October 2024, new statutory guidance was published, and the government will be trialling a kinship allowance in England. This guide will help you identify what you can expect as a kinship carer and what to do if you do not receive the support you need.

Lastly, I want to encourage you that you are not alone on this journey. There are local kinship peer support groups with people going through similar issues as you. You can also contact the amazing and supportive staff at Kinship through the advice line. Or take part in free training workshops. Visit **kinship.org.uk** to find out about all of these offers and more.

Keith Whittaker
Dad to 2 amazing kinship daughters and 5 other children
Volunteer at Kinship

About Kinship

We are Kinship. The leading kinship care charity in England and Wales. We're here for kinship carers – friends or family who step up to raise a child when their parents aren't able to.

We are made by and for our community of kinship carers. For too long they have been isolated without the help they need.

Our purpose is to change lives, and change the system. We support, advise and inform kinship carers. Connecting them so they feel empowered. Because a child needs the love and warmth of a thriving family.

We develop research, campaigns and policy solutions. Creating positive change across society. Because for kinship families, love alone is not enough.

And as we see momentum building for change, we keep working with our community and making impact.

Join us. Together, let's commit to change for kinship families.

Find out more at **kinship.org.uk**

About this guide

"

If I'd had the guide at the beginning it would have been like a bible to me. I would have valued it like that. Online is great, but having it in one place, physically, is really helpful.

Kinship carer

Becoming a kinship carer can feel daunting, but it can be a really rewarding experience for you, as well as for the child you are caring for.

Kinship carers have stepped up to care for more than 132,000 children in England. Getting the help and support you need can seem complicated, overwhelming and confusing. You may feel like you're alone, but you're not. This guide is designed to help you navigate your journey.

You can use this guide alongside our other services including our website, peer support services, our advice line and our programme of training and workshops. You can find a full list of Kinship's services and a list of helpful organisations in chapter 15.

Contact Kinship's advice line

You can call us for free on **0300 123 7015**

For more information, including our opening hours visit **kinship.org.uk/advice-line**

We've spoken to kinship carers to help make this updated edition as practical and useful as possible. We've included checklists and questions you can take to support providers, and space for you to make your own notes. It aims to help you understand your rights and responsibilities, and the things you need to consider when you're stepping in to care for someone else's child. We have included information on topics that kinship carers told us would be helpful.

This guide covers:

- the different types of kinship care

- things you might want to consider as a kinship carer – like housing and accommodation, practical and emotional support

- living as a kinship carer – including managing family relationships and contact, the education system and financial support

- sources of support and further information

In writing this guide, we have aimed to make the language as accessible as possible. Kinship carers have told us that there's lots of new words, terms and phrases to understand. To help you navigate this, we've put together a glossary of terms that might be unfamiliar at the end of this guide in chapter 16. We have also used best practice from sites such as **GOV.UK** to improve readability of the guide. An example of this means we have been purposeful about using numbers instead of words – like 7 rather than seven.

We refer to 'kinship care' as an umbrella term for anyone who looks after the child of a family member or friend. You'll also see other organisations refer to kinship care as 'family and friends' care. Kinship carers might be referred to as 'connected carers', 'kinship foster carers' or 'special guardians'.

Throughout the guide we've used the term 'your child' or 'the child in your care', but know that in many cases, you might be looking after multiple children, including your own. The child you care for might also be a young person or teenager.

The guide is based on the law in England, so although many of the general issues are the same elsewhere in the UK, the rights and responsibilities of kinship carers will be different.

We have taken a content design approach to creating this edition of the Kinship Care Guide for England. Content design is a research-led approach to creating content that effectively communicates information and meets people's needs.

The content designers that worked on this edition are:

- Katie Connolly, former Senior Content Designer, Kinship

- Rachel Nelligan, Senior Content Designer, Kinship

The process of updating this guide was overseen by Lauren Plüss, former Head of Digital and Content at Kinship.

1. What is kinship care?

Key points in this chapter:

- kinship carers play a significant role in caring for children who cannot live with their parents

- there are different types of kinship care, from informal arrangements to legal arrangements like special guardianship

- different types of kinship care bring different rights, responsibilities and opportunities for support

- as a kinship carer, you and the children in your care may face particular challenges

- your local authority or council's kinship local offer should include services to help you as a kinship carer

Kinship care is when a child lives full-time or most of the time with a relative or close family friend. This is usually because their parents are not able to care for them. It can be a temporary or permanent arrangement.

There are different types of kinship care. You may become a different type of kinship carer as your situation changes over time. Your rights, responsibilities and the support you can get will depend on your specific circumstances.

The National Kinship Care Strategy for England

In December 2023, the UK government launched the first ever national strategy for kinship care.

The strategy included a commitment to updating statutory guidance on kinship care for local authorities, which was published by the Department for Education in October 2024. This is called Kinship care: statutory guidance for local authorities and can be found on GOV.UK.

Statutory guidance is given by the government to local authorities to help them follow what the law says they should do. They should follow this guidance unless there is a good reason not to. More information on the statutory guidance is in chapter 13.

A new National Kinship Care Ambassador has also been appointed. This new role will advocate for kinship children and carers across government and work directly with local authorities to improve services.

You can read the full strategy on **GOV.UK** by searching 'National Kinship Care Strategy for England'.

It includes a commitment to a new government definition of kinship care to be used in statutory guidance. We've included it here.

Definition of kinship care

1 Kinship care is any situation in which a child is being raised in the care of a friend or family member who is not their parent. The arrangement may be temporary or longer term.

2 The following are all types of kinship care arrangement, however this list is not exhaustive:

a. informal kinship care arrangements (not approved foster care) including:

i. a private family arrangement in which a close relative who does not hold parental responsibility, raises the child and

- the local authority has had no major role in making the arrangement for the child; and

- where a family court has not made an order in respect to the care of the child.

ii. where a child under the age of 16 is being provided with accommodation for less than 28 days by an individual in their own home who is not a close relative

iii. where a 16 or 17-year-old is being provided with accommodation by an individual who is not a close relative in their own home

b. a private fostering arrangement in which someone who is not a close relative* of the child looks after the child for 28 days or more** (as per section 66(1)(a) and (b) of the Children Act 1989)***

c. where a 'lives with' child arrangements order**** has been granted in respect of the child, in favour of someone who is a friend or family member but is not the child's parent.

d. where a special guardianship order has been granted appointing a friend or family member as the child's special guardian.

e. where a child is a 'looked after child' by virtue of either an interim or final care order or being accommodated by the local authority (usually under

Definition of kinship care *continued*

section 20 of the Children Act 1989) and each of the following apply (this may be described as 'kinship foster care' or 'family and friends foster care'):

i. the child is being cared for by a friend or family member who is not their parent, and

ii. the friend or family member is approved as a local authority foster carer either on a temporary basis or following full assessment.

f. where an adoption order has been granted in respect of the child and, prior to the making of the order, the adopter was a friend or family member.

*In relation to private fostering, "relative" has the meaning given in section 105 of the Children Act 1989. It includes only the following: grandparent, brother, sister, uncle or aunt (whether full blood or half blood or by marriage or civil partnership), and step-parent (a married step-parent, including a civil partner).

**For the purposes of this kinship definition, the term private fostering arrangement includes only individuals accommodating a child. It does not apply to organisations or bodies.

***16- and 17-year-olds who are disabled will be deemed to be in a private fostering arrangement.

****Pursuant to section 8 of the Children Act 1989.

Who is a kinship carer?

You are a kinship carer if you are looking after the child of a relative or friend on a full-time basis. It could be a temporary or permanent arrangement, for any reason.

Kinship carers can be:

- grandparents
- brothers or sisters
- aunts or uncles
- people who know the child well, who aren't related

It also includes people who are related to a child by marriage or civil partnership. For example, a parent's husband or wife or stepbrothers and stepsisters. Legally, a 'relative' is defined by the Children Act 1989 as someone who is not the child's parent but is a sibling, aunt, uncle, grandparent or step-parent.

Kinship care might also be called:

- family and friends care
- informal kinship care
- private foster care
- special guardianship
- connected care

You might see some of these terms in official documents or policies.

Following the publication of the kinship care strategy in December 2023, the government will replace use of the term 'family and friends care' with 'kinship care' in future government guidance. We would expect local policies to be updated to reflect this, although it may take some time.

There are different types of kinship care

Some kinship care arrangements are informal and arranged privately within the family. Others might include more formal, legal arrangements involving the family court and your local authority.

The responsibilities you have, and the support you are eligible to receive, will be different depending on the type of kinship care arrangement you are in. As circumstances change it is quite possible that the type of kinship carer you are might also change.

Kinship care can mean:

Informal kinship care

An informal kinship care arrangement is where a close relative looks after a child. In some circumstances this could also be a more distant relative or friend. See chapter 2 for more details.

Overall responsibility for the child stays with the parents (called 'parental responsibility'). They are not in the care of your local authority's children's services department.

The child's parents and kinship carers agree together how the arrangement works.

Read more in chapter 2

Private foster care

Private foster care is when someone who is not a child's parent or close relative looks after them for 28 days or more.

Arrangements are agreed by you and the parent, but you will have to notify the local authority and undergo a short assessment.

You may be asked to make day-to-day decisions, but the parents keep full responsibility for the child.

Read more in chapter 3

Kinship foster care

Kinship foster care is when a family member or friend becomes a child's approved foster carer. It is sometimes called family and friends foster care.

You must be assessed and approved as a foster carer. The child is in the care of children's services, who share parental responsibility with the child's parents.

Unlike other types of kinship care, you will receive a regular foster care allowance.

Read more in chapter 4

Child arrangements orders

A child arrangements order is a legal order given by a family court. You might see this referred to as a CAO. Child arrangements orders replaced residence orders in 2014. Information about child arrangements orders in this guide also apply to people holding residence orders.

They usually last until the child is 18 years old, and you share parental responsibility with their parents.

You can make day-to-day decisions without needing the parents' permission, but must include them in any big decisions about the child.

Read more in chapter 5

Special guardianship orders

A special guardianship order is a legal order given by a family court. You might see this referred to as a SGO.

When you become a special guardian, the child will live with you until they are 18 years old.

You share parental responsibility with the child's parents but can make nearly all major decisions about the child without the parents' involvement.

Read more in chapter 6

Adoption

Adoption is not appropriate or recommended for most kinship carers. When you adopt a child, the link between the child and their parents is legally and permanently broken. It changes family arrangements forever. As an adopter, you gain complete parental responsibility for the child.

Read more in chapter 7

Living with testamentary guardians

A testamentary guardian is someone who has been appointed formally in writing by a parent or special guardian. If there is no one else with parental responsibility, the testamentary guardian gains parental responsibility upon the parent or special guardian's death.

If you are a testamentary guardian, you might want to seek legal advice to ensure you understand your rights and options.

See chapter 15 for organisations that can help.

As you navigate what type of kinship care arrangement might be the right one for you, the checklists we've put together in the below chapters might help you to understand the different rights, responsibilities and support available to you:

- chapter 13, working with your local authority children's services – includes a checklist of questions you could ask children's services

- chapter 14, the legal process – includes a checklist of questions you could ask a solicitor

Parental responsibility and the different types of kinship care

Some of the key differences in the types of kinship care relate to parental responsibility, and who has it.

Parental responsibility (sometimes called PR) is the rights, responsibilites, duties, powers and authority that a parent has in relation to a child and their property.

Whatever your circumstances as a kinship carer, it's important to understand what decisions you can make and what rights the child's parent has.

If there is a legal order in place (such as a child arrangements order, special guardianship order or care order), you share parental responsibility with the parents and possibly the local authority. Testamentary guardians will only gain parental responsibility if there are no other individuals with parental responsibility, such as another parent or special guardian.

If you are a kinship foster carer, the local authority will identify in a placement plan who can make which decisions. It's usually referred to as arrangements for 'delegated authority'.

If you don't have parental responsibility, it can make everyday decisions difficult depending on your relationship with the parents. You might struggle to come to agreements with the parents, or need regular contact to get their consent, such as for school trips.

Read more about parental responsibility and making decisions for the child in each type of kinship care chapter, and more in chapter 8 on becoming a kinship carer.

Children Act 1989

The Children Act 1989 is the law relating to protecting children in England and Wales. It aims to ensure that every child is kept safe and protected from harm, and their developmental needs are met. It is the basis of law for most children's services duties and responsibilities to children and their families. It is made up of a range of sections which cover different areas.

You will see the Children Act 1989 or various sections referred to throughout this guide, as it's central to your rights as a kinship carer and outlines the responsibilities of children's services.

The different types of kinship care

This table highlights the key features of different forms of kinship care, to help you compare and make any decisions.

Refer to the relevant sections of the guide for more information, checklists and key questions to ask.

	Informal kinship care	Private foster care	Kinship foster care
You are	A close relative: legally the child's grandparent, brother, sister, uncle, aunt or step-parent.	Someone who knows or is connected with the child but is not a close relative.	A family member, family friend or someone else closely connected to a child that is in the care of children's services.
Arranged by	You and the child's parent(s). It is **not** made by the local authority.	You and the child's parent(s).	You and the local authority for a child in the care of children's services.
Approved by	No one: it is a family arrangement.	Under 28 days, no one. Notify your local children's services department if the arrangement will last more than 28 days. They will carry out an assessment.	Children's services should assess and approve you as a foster carer. Temporary approval can be given in an emergency.
Lasts for	As long as you and the parents agree. It may be ended by you or the child's parents.	As long as you and the parents agree. It may be ended by you, the child's parents or children's services.	As long as you and children's services agree, as set out in your foster care agreement, placement plan and looked-after child plan.
Supervised and reviewed by	No one.	No one officially, but children's services will review the arrangement.	A social worker will visit and children's services will review. Approval is reviewed annually.

	Child arrangements order	Special guardianship order	Adoption
You are	A carer seeking parental responsibility, who the child has lived with for at least a year, or 3 years for private foster carers.	A carer seeking a permanent arrangement with overriding parental responsibility, who the child has lived with for at least a year, or 3 years for private foster carers.	A relative the child has lived with for at least 3 of the last 5 years. A kinship foster carer who the child has lived with for at least a year.
Arranged by	Applying to the court. If the child is in the care of children's services, you will need to notify them, and a social worker will be involved too.	Applying to the court. Children's services and a social worker will be involved too.	Applying to the court. You need the consent of the parents, or to demonstrate why this isn't needed or suitable.
Approved by	The court.	The local authority will assess your ability to care for the child but the court decides.	The local authority will assess your ability to care for the child but the court decides.
Lasts for	Until the child reaches 18 unless the court changes anything before then.	Until the child reaches 18.	Adoption is a permanent lifelong arrangement.
Supervised and reviewed by	No one.	No one.	No one. A social worker will supervise after you apply and until the adoption order is made, but not after.

	Informal kinship care	Private foster care	Kinship foster care
Your rights and responsibilities	To safeguard and promote the child's welfare. You do not have parental responsibility.	To tell the local authority that you are a private foster carer. You do not have parental responsibility.	Set out in a foster care agreement and placement plan. You do not have parental responsibility.
The parents' rights and responsibilities	Full parental responsibility.	Full parental responsibility. They should tell children's services about the private fostering arrangement.	Full parental responsibility. For a looked-after child, the local authority also has parental responsibility and can limit decisions made by parents.
Additional support you can get	No specific support. You may be able to get support from your local authority for a child assessed as in need.	Possible support from a social worker. You may be able to get support from your local authority for a child assessed as in need.	A health plan, personal education plan, contact plan and placement plan for the child. Training, advice and practical support for you.
Financial support you might get	Benefits for families, such as Child Benefit. Guardian's Allowance (if one/both parents has died). One-off payments for a child in need.	Benefits for families, such as Child Benefit. Guardian's Allowance (if one/both parents has died). One-off payments for a child in need.	Foster care allowance. A fee to recognise the carers' commitment, in some fostering services. You cannot claim child benefit, child tax credit or Guardian's Allowance.
Read more detail on this arrangement	Chapter 2 Informal kinship care	Chapter 3 Private foster care	Chapter 4 Kinship foster care

	Child arrangements order	Special guardianship order	Adoption
Your rights and responsibilities	Shared parental responsibility with the parents. The parents need to be consulted over major decisions.	Shared parental responsibility with the parents. However, you are able to make almost all decisions about the child without the parents' consent.	All the rights and responsibilities of parents.
The parents' rights and responsibilities	Shared parental responsibility with the child arrangements order holder.	Shared parental responsibility with the special guardian, but the guardian can make almost all decisions without the parents' involvement.	None: the birth parents are no longer legally related to the child.
Additional support you can get	No specific support. You may be able to get support from your local authority for a child assessed as in need.	An assessment for support services by children's services.	An assessment for support services by children's services.
Financial support you might get	Benefits for families, such as Child Benefit. Guardian's Allowance (if one/both parents has died). Child arrangements order allowance, in some circumstances.	Benefits for families, such as Child Benefit. Guardian's Allowance (if one/both parents has died). An assessment for support services by children's services if the child was previously in their care. If they were not looked-after, you can ask for an assessment but it is not guaranteed.	Benefits for families, such as Child Benefit. An assessment for support services by children's services if the child was previously in their care.
Read more detail on this arrangement	Chapter 5 Child arrangements orders	Chapter 6 Special guardianship orders	Chapter 7 Adoption

Adapted from Annex A to *Family and Friends Care: Statutory Guidance for Local Authorities* (Department for Education 2011)

Kinship local offer

Guidance published by the Department for Education in 2024 states that local authorities should provide visible, accessible and up-to-date information for kinship carers on the support available to them, detailed in their 'kinship local offer'. It might also be known as a family and friends care policy, a connected care policy or kinship care policy.

It should explain some of the legal rights and responsibilities of being a kinship carer. You will see the kinship local offer referred to throughout this guide, as it's a key document that will help you understand the support available from your local authority depending on your kinship care arrangement.

You can find out more about the kinship local offer in chapter 13: working with your local authority children's services.

The positive impact of kinship care

There are clear benefits for both children and their carers in keeping children within their family network. Carers often say the rewards are enormous for them, and they would make no other choice but to step in when needed.

Kinship carers can build on their existing relationship with the child to help them feel loved and cared for. This helps them grow up and develop as happy children. Kinship carers often have a special bond with the children which helps them to stick with things through difficult periods.

Staying within their wider family can be much less disruptive for children than living with foster carers they don't know. It can help minimise the child's sense of loss and retains their sense of identity. Kinship carers often have close relationships with the child's parents and can tell stories of their childhoods. This can positively impact the child's identity development.

Children will usually find it easier to form an attachment to a kinship carer than to someone they didn't know before. It is also usually possible for them to keep in contact with other family members and their parents, even when they have been through traumatic experiences.

Sometimes it is also easier for children to explain their situation to their friends – 'living with auntie/uncle/grandparents' may feel simpler for them to explain than 'in foster care'.

What children want

Most children want their parents to be supported to care for them, or if necessary, to live with members of their extended family, rather than be taken into the care of children's services.

They sometimes feel their families should be given better opportunities to suggest other ways of looking after them before they go into care.

When they do have to be taken into the care of children's services, most children would prefer to be placed with someone from their own family, but this isn't always the case.

"She always cared for me, looked after me and we had a lot of fun. My grandparents used to record the things we did together, days out and zoos, play dates and activities with friends and all that. They liked to keep the memories. We've still got them all now."
Young person raised in kinship care

Next steps

- read the in-depth chapter relating to your specific kinship care arrangement (chapters 2-7)
- find out what support Kinship can provide you with as you become a kinship carer (at the start of chapter 15)

Find support in your area

You can use Kinship Compass, our postcode search tool, to find local services to support you as a kinship carer.

Enter your location or postcode to find useful support and services near you including:

- support groups
- local authority teams and contact details
- your local kinship offer or family and friends care policy
- your virtual school
- your nearest legal advice clinic

Visit **kinship.org.uk/in-your-area**

2. Informal kinship care

Key points in this chapter:

- informal arrangements are made between members of the child's family or friends, usually between parents and the kinship carers

- if you are a close relative there is no legal requirement to inform the local authority

- the child is not in the care of the local authority or children's services, if they are, the arrangement is not informal

- a social worker does not place the child in an informal arrangement, but might offer some support and guidance

- informal kinship carers do not have a legal order, do not have parental responsibility and cannot make decisions without parental agreement

- the parents can end the arrangement at any time, but if you are concerned about returning the child to their parents, contact children's services, or the police

- there is no specific financial support for informal kinship carers, but you may be entitled to benefits for families such as Child Benefit

What is informal kinship care?

Informal kinship care is when the local authority has no major involvement, there is no court order in place and when the carer is either:

- a close relative taking care of a child on behalf of their parents

- a more distant relative or family friend taking care of a non-disabled young person aged 16 or 17, or

- a more distant relative or family friend taking care of a child under 16 for less than 28 days

In all other situations where the carer is not a close relative, the local authority do not have major involvement and there is no court order in place, it should be a private foster care arrangement.

If you are a close relative of the child, there is no requirement to notify the local authority about the arrangement, unless you want to do so to seek additional support.

Kinship care is sometimes arranged informally at first. It may lead to a more formal arrangement, like a special guardianship order. This could happen months or years later, depending on the circumstances.

Informal kinship care can arise when:

The parent arranges for you to look after their child because they're not able to

A child's parents might ask you to care for their child. In difficult circumstances, you might offer to help. For instance, a parent arranges for you to look after their child while they're in hospital or recovering from an illness. After recovery, the plan would be for that the child to return to live with them.

An older child or teenager might choose to come and live with you

The parents might later agree, but it is not always simple. Whatever the reason, it's up to the parent to decide that the arrangements are suitable for their child. Seek advice from Kinship, the police, or your local authority if you need it.

This arrangement does not involve any kind of legal order. The local authority's children's services do not have any responsibilities for the child.

Are you an informal kinship carer or a foster carer?

Local children's services should support and assess you as a kinship foster carer (see chapter 4) if:

- children's services say that the child cannot return to their parents care or,
- children's services say they must supervise any contact they have with the parents

In this case you should seek legal advice, a list of organisations is available in chapter 15.

Only a close relative can be an informal kinship carer for more than 28 days

A close relative is legally defined as the child's grandparent, brother, sister, uncle or aunt. This includes people who are relatives by half blood, marriage or civil partnership and step-parents.

If the care is arranged with a more distant relative or family friend, the arrangement is for more than 28 days, and the child is 16 or under, it is private foster care (see chapter 3).

The arrangement is made between you and the child's family

Children's services are not involved in informal kinship care arrangements. But, if you or children's services think that additional support may be necessary to safeguard or promote the child's welfare, they may become involved.

Your rights and responsibilities

You have a responsibility to safeguard and promote the child's welfare. But, parents still have a legal responsibility for their children. Ideally, you need to work in partnership with them in the best interests of the child. If it's hard to get the parents' agreement for any reason, you can ask children's services for advice.

Parents are still responsible for decision making

Parents still have parental responsibility. This means they are responsible for financial support and for making decisions about their child.

They can delegate day-to-day decision making to the kinship carer. But, they must consent to major decisions such as:

- medical treatment (except in an emergency where the hospital will decide the best course of treatment)

- schooling

- foreign travel

- hair cuts

The Children Act 1989 (section 3 (5)) says that even if you're not a child's parent or legal guardian, you can still make decisions to keep them safe. If you're looking after a child, you're allowed to do what makes sense and is reasonable to keep them safe and healthy.

To clarify which decisions you can make, you might find it helpful to draw up a document which you and the parents sign. If you have trouble arranging this with the parents, you can ask children's services for support. See more information on becoming a kinship carer in chapter 8.

Parents can decide whether the informal kinship care arrangement should continue.

Longer term arrangements

As an informal kinship carer, you might want to consider applying for a legal order to gain a greater degree of parental responsibility. It is also a way of providing a more secure and certain family situation for the child. See chapter 5 on child arrangements orders and chapter 6 on special guardianship orders.

Without a legal order, informal kinship care arrangements can end when the parent decides. The parent can resume care without giving you notice, no matter how long you've been caring for the child.

If you are not a close relative and there are plans for the child to be with you for longer than 28 days, then this counts as private foster care. You will need to notify your local authority. See chapter 3.

If you no longer wish to or cannot continue with the arrangement, you should speak to the parents.

If you are concerned that returning the child to their parents could put them at risk, then speak to children's services as soon as possible.

Peggy and her grandchildren

Ross and Alex, aged 14 and 15, are living with their grandmother Peggy. Their mother has leukemia and has periods in and out of hospital.

Even when she is out of hospital, she finds running a home very tiring. Peggy and her daughter have a good relationship and feel that it is less disruptive for the boys to be with their grandmother.

Peggy feels that applying for a legal order is unnecessary and would upset her daughter. In any case the boys are approaching an age when they can make decisions for themselves.

Peggy is a pensioner and is claiming Child Benefit and the child element in Universal Credit to support the boys.

Support you can get

If you're very worried about the child's health and development, or if they have a disability, you can ask your local children's services to assess them as a child in need. See chapter 13 for more information about the definition of a child in need and support under section 17 of the Children Act 1989.

You can also ask a doctor, GP or health visitor to ask children's services on your behalf.

You can access other support through early help services. Search your local authority's website for 'early help'. You can ask the child's school or health visitor to help with this.

You can also ask the local authority if they know of any local support groups for informal carers. Kinship provide a range of support services for informal kinship carers.

There are lots of organisations along with Kinship who can provide support in different areas. Find helpful organisations in chapter 15.

Benefits and financial support

There is no specific financial support for informal kinship carers. In an informal kinship care arrangement, the child's parents must provide financial support.

You may be entitled to:

- Guardian's Allowance (if one/both parents have died)
- one-off payments for a child in need, see section 17 support in chapter 12

You may also be able to access other benefits, for example benefits for families. This could include Child Benefit, the child element in Universal Credit if you're of working age or Pension Credit if you're of pension age.

For information on what you can claim, see chapter 12 on benefits and financial support.

Notes

3. Private foster care

Key points in this chapter:

- private foster care is an arrangement between you and the child's parent that is intended to last more than 28 consecutive days

- private foster carers are not a close relative of the child, but know or are connected to them

- parents can end the arrangement at any time

- private foster carers do not have parental responsibility

- the term 'private foster care' can be confusing, it is different to foster care arranged by children's services

- private foster carers don't receive a foster care allowance

- the local authority does not approve private foster carers, but it does assess the suitability of the arrangements

- a social worker will pay regular visits

What is private foster care?

Private foster care is care by someone who knows or was connected with the child before they started to care for them but is not a close relative. The Children Act 1989 defines a relative as someone who is not the child's parent but is a sibling, aunt, uncle, grandparent or step-parent.

Private foster carers are often distant relatives or family friends.

The term 'private fostering' can be confusing, as it is different to foster care arranged by children's services.

The child is not placed by the local authority in a private fostering arrangement.

Private foster care applies to children:

- under 16 (or up to 18 if the child is disabled)
- not in the care of children's services

If the child is 16 or 17, and is not disabled, it would be an informal arrangement (see chapter 2).

Private foster care is an arrangement which lasts (or is intended to last) for more than 28 consecutive days. If it lasts less than 28 days, it is an informal arrangement. However, if you are asked to look after the child for periods of less than 28 days but several times over a period of a few months, you should contact your local children's services and ask about their policy.

Jade and her friend's children

Jade looked after Courtney, 6, and Sean, 3 while their mum Susan was in prison serving a 12-week sentence for shoplifting.

Jade had been close friends with Susan since they were at school. Susan had arranged for Jade to look after the children for a few days during her court case. She did not expect to go to prison, and didn't make any further plans.

As the arrangement was now going to last for more than 28 days, Jade had to inform children's services that she was looking after Courtney and Sean. She was entitled to receive any government benefits for the period she was looking after the children.

While in her care, Jade was able to make day-to-day decisions about the children, but big decisions, such as a school application or holiday abroad, needed to be agreed by Susan.

Staying with Jade during this time meant the children could be with someone they had an existing relationship with, rather than be in foster care with a stranger. Once Susan left prison, she was able to take the children back to live with her.

The arrangement is made between you and the child's parents

Children's services are not involved in making private foster arrangements, but they do need to be informed.

If children's services are involved in placing the child with you, or a social worker is saying that they are unable to return a child to their parents, this is not private fostering. You will need to be assessed, paid an allowance and supported as a kinship foster carer (see chapter 4).

Your rights and responsibilities

You need to let children's services know that you plan to become a private foster carer. But in many situations, this will happen in an emergency.

Tell them as soon as possible if the arrangement has already started. You must, legally, tell them within 6 weeks of the child living with you.

Ideally, inform them 6 weeks before the arrangement starts.

You'll be asked to provide information about:

- the child
- their parents
- the planned duration of the arrangement

Children's services should give you information about private fostering in their kinship local offer.

Find your local authority's kinship local offer (previously family and friends care policy) and other local information, services and support on our postcode search tool, Kinship Compass: **kinship.org.uk/in-your-area**

Parents are still responsible for decision making

Parents have a duty to notify the local authority that they are arranging for their child to live with a private foster carer.

Parents still have parental responsibility. This means they are responsible for financial support and for making decisions about their child.

They can delegate day-to-day decision making to you as a kinship carer. But they must consent to major decisions such as:

- medical treatment (except in an emergency where the hospital will make a decision on the best course of treatment)
- schooling
- foreign travel
- hair cuts

The Children Act 1989 says that even if you're not a child's parent or legal guardian, you can still make decisions to keep them safe. If you're looking after a child, you're allowed to do what makes sense and is reasonable to keep them safe and healthy.

To clarify which decisions you can make, you might find it helpful to draw up a document which you both sign. If you have trouble arranging this with the parents, you can ask children's services for support. You can also ask Kinship for advice. See chapter 8 for more information on decision-making for the child in your care.

Parents can decide whether the kinship care arrangement should continue.

You need to notify the local authority about your arrangement

Once you notify the local authority that you have become a private foster carer, they will arrange for a social worker from children's services to visit you and also meet the child.

It is a good idea to be open with children's services and share relevant information with them.

You do not need to be formally approved as a foster carer, but the social worker will check some things about the arrangement, including:

- if the carer or anyone living in the house has a relevant criminal record, this is called a Disclosure and Barring Service (DBS) check

- accommodation

- who else lives in the household

- arrangements for contact with the parents

- school

- health

A **Disclosure and Barring Service (DBS)** check is a way for children's services to check details of any spent and unspent convictions, cautions, final warnings or reprimands. There are different types of DBS checks from basic to enhanced with a check of the barred lists.

You, and any other household members over 18 (sometimes 16), would require an enhanced DBS check if you're considering becoming a private foster carer.

The social worker will also visit the child's parents as part of their assessment.

The arrangement can last until you or the parents decide

Private fostering arrangements can be ended whenever the parent decides and without notice.

If you are unable or unwilling to continue looking after the child, it's up to the parents to arrange alternative care, but you should also inform children's services.

It doesn't matter how long you have cared for the child: their parent can still resume care without giving you notice.

You may think there are strong reasons why it would be better for the child to stay with you rather than return to their parents. If so, you should consider applying for a child arrangements order or special guardianship order. This will formalise your arrangement. For more information see chapter 5 on child arrangements orders and chapter 6 on special guardianship orders.

A social worker will supervise and review the arrangement

A social worker is required to visit the child you are privately fostering at least every 6 weeks during the first year, and then at least every 12 weeks after that. Visits can be announced or unannounced. You, the child or the parent can request additional visits.

The social worker should give you advice and support to help you care for the child. They should also build a positive relationship with the child.

Children who are privately fostered may also be assessed as children 'in need' and provided with family services support by the local authority. You can ask your social worker for an assessment.

Benefits and financial support

There is no specific financial support for private foster carers. In most cases, the child's parents must provide financial support, though we often find that they are unable or do not want to. It can be helpful to discuss with the parents what financial support they are able to give for the period of time you are looking after the child. You might want to put this in writing to make sure you both agree.

You may be entitled to:

- Guardian's Allowance (if one/both parents has died)
- one-off payments for a child in need, see section 17 support in chapter 12

You may also be able to access other benefits, for example benefits for families. This could include Child Benefit, the child element in Universal Credit if you're of working age or Pension Credit if you're of pension age.

For information on what you can claim, see chapter 12 on benefits and financial support.

Are you a private foster carer?

This chart will help you determine if you need to inform your local authority about a private foster care arrangement.

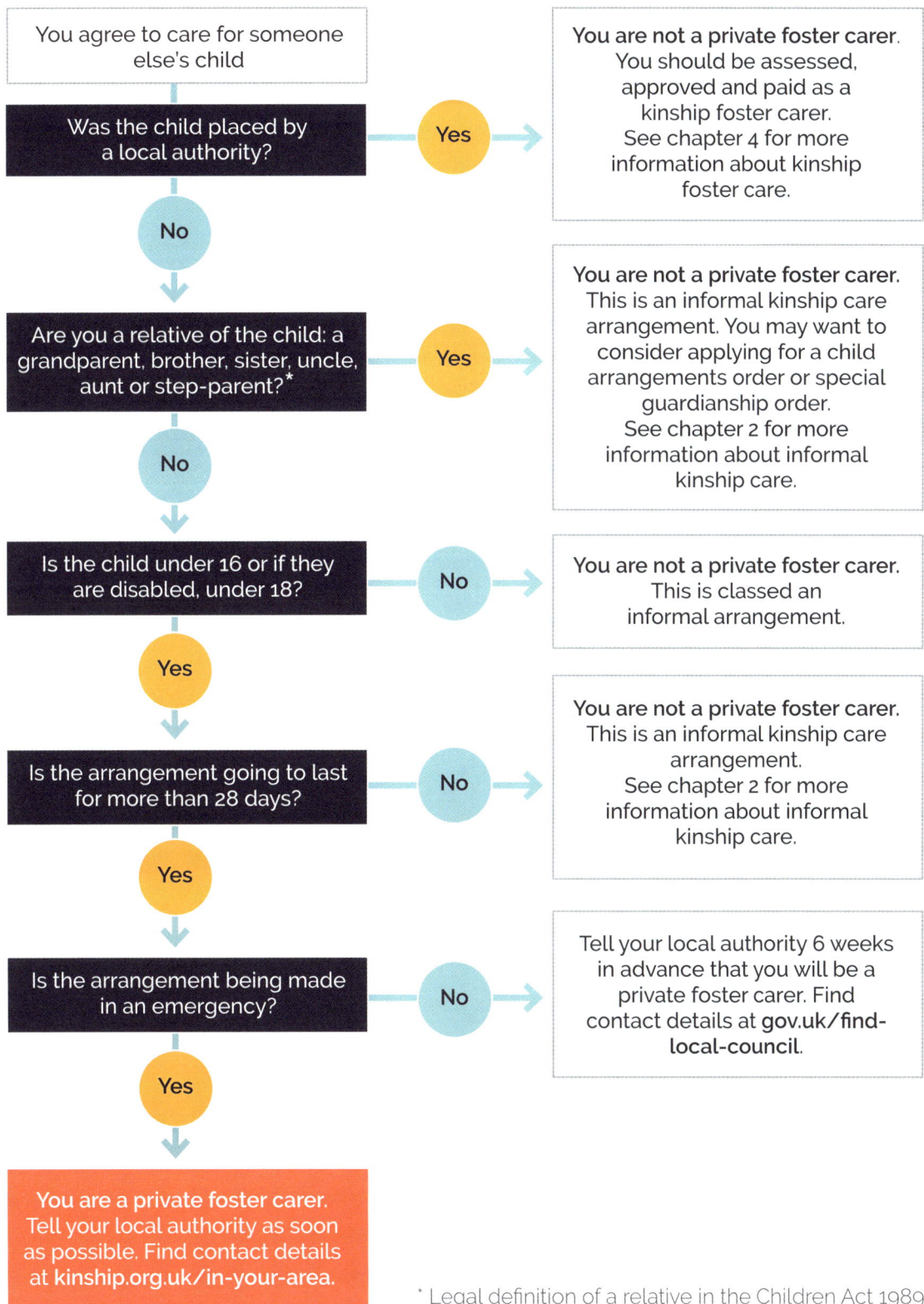

You agree to care for someone else's child

Was the child placed by a local authority?

Yes → **You are not a private foster carer.** You should be assessed, approved and paid as a kinship foster carer. See chapter 4 for more information about kinship foster care.

No ↓

Are you a relative of the child: a grandparent, brother, sister, uncle, aunt or step-parent?*

Yes → **You are not a private foster carer.** This is an informal kinship care arrangement. You may want to consider applying for a child arrangements order or special guardianship order. See chapter 2 for more information about informal kinship care.

No ↓

Is the child under 16 or if they are disabled, under 18?

No → **You are not a private foster carer.** This is classed an informal arrangement.

Yes ↓

Is the arrangement going to last for more than 28 days?

No → **You are not a private foster carer.** This is an informal kinship care arrangement. See chapter 2 for more information about informal kinship care.

Yes ↓

Is the arrangement being made in an emergency?

No → Tell your local authority 6 weeks in advance that you will be a private foster carer. Find contact details at **gov.uk/find-local-council**.

Yes ↓

You are a private foster carer. Tell your local authority as soon as possible. Find contact details at kinship.org.uk/in-your-area.

* Legal definition of a relative in the Children Act 1989

4. Kinship foster care

Key points in this chapter:

- kinship foster care is when a local authority children's services department places a child with someone that is a family member, family friend or someone else closely connected to them

- it is sometimes known as family and friends foster care or connected person foster care

- children may be in the care of children's services by agreement with the parents, or because of a court order

- kinship carers who are looking after a child in the care of children's services must be approved as foster carers. Temporary approval can be granted in an emergency

- kinship foster carers do not have parental responsibility

- you will have a supervising social worker who provides ongoing review and support

- the child also has a social worker

- kinship foster carers are entitled to receive the same foster care allowances and fees as other foster carers within that local authority

What is kinship foster care?

Kinship foster care is when children's services place a child in their care with a family member, family friend or someone else closely connected to them. It is also known as family and friends foster care or connected person foster care. You do not have parental responsibility as a kinship foster carer.

The child is in the care of children's services, either through:

- a voluntary agreement with their parents

- an interim care order, full care order, or emergency protection order made by a family court

When a child is in their care, children's services decide where they will live. They will always try to place the child with a relative, friend or another connected person if it is in their best interests. However, that person must be assessed and approved as a foster carer.

It is important to know that if children's services do not consider it safe to send the child home, then it is not an informal care arrangement. You should be assessed, supported and paid an allowance as a kinship foster carer. If a social worker was involved in the arrangement, then you may be able to challenge children's services and ask that the child has a looked after status. Anyone under the age 18 who is in the care of the local authority, either because their parents have agreed or by an order of the court is a looked-after child. This means there will be additional support for the child from the local authority.

Paula and her nieces

Paula is the full-time carer of her 3 nieces aged 7, 11 and 13. Her younger sister wasn't coping after moving away from her neighbourhood to escape a violent relationship, and was struggling with addiction.

Children's services agreed to accommodate the girls and Paula was approved as a foster carer. Paula moved into a flat found for her by them.

She receives allowances as a foster carer, the support of a social worker and has attended training courses for foster carers to help with the challenges of parenting looked-after children.

The girls' behaviour has improved significantly in Paula's care and their mother is meeting targets set for her to become drug free. The girls are now spending more time with their mum with a view to returning home in the next few months.

Children's services make the arrangements

When a child is in the care of children's services, they have to decide what placement is the most appropriate to meet the child's needs.

The law requires children's services to give preference to a placement with a family member or friend who is approved as a foster carer.

You can ask your supervising social worker to give you information about what the process will be.

Fostering assessment

When children's services place a child with you, they should arrange a fostering assessment.

The assessment will include checks on you, your home and your history and background. It can feel intrusive and can be a difficult process to go through.

You might be assessed as a suitable carer in all ways except your housing situation. In this case, children's services should support you to improve your situation so you can care for the child.

See more detail in the section on the fostering assessment process later in this chapter.

If a child is placed with you in an emergency

Sometimes there is no time to carry out a full fostering assessment before placing the child with you. Children's services can give you temporary approval as a foster carer for up to 16 weeks to allow time for a full fostering assessment.

Occasionally, temporary approval can be extended by 8 weeks, but no longer. Children's services may decide it is better to place the child with an approved foster carer, short term, while they assess your suitability.

Your rights and responsibilities

Kinship foster carers do not have parental responsibility. Children's services are responsible for the care of a looked-after child, even though you are providing this care as a foster carer.

Children's services could remove the child from your care without going to court if they felt there was a risk of significant harm to them.

All foster carers must sign a foster care agreement. This clarifies your role and responsibilities, as well as the support you will be given by the local authority fostering service.

You will need to make basic day-to-day decisions about the child, but would need to consult children's services over major decisions such as:

- medical treatment (except in an emergency where the hospital will make a decision on the best course of treatment)
- schooling
- foreign travel
- hair cuts

The Children Act 1989 says that even if you're not a child's parent or legal guardian, you can still make decisions to keep them safe. If you're looking after a child, you're allowed to do what makes sense and is reasonable to keep them safe and healthy.

You are expected to work with social workers, teachers, and health workers to provide the best possible care and support to the child. You will have to allow social worker visits, and might be asked to complete a diary or log book for the child.

You'll need to agree and sign a placement plan

Placement plans will set out which decisions can be made by you or need to be referred to the social worker or parent (called delegated authority).

Both you and the child should be involved in creating the plan. Normally the child's parents or other family members are involved too. A meeting is usually held for this purpose.

The placement plan is important because it says how you are expected to care for the child, as well as what other people will do to support you in this.

It also records the arrangements for:

- education and health

- contact arrangements with the child's family

- the child's finances, such as pocket money and savings

Ideally foster carers can make the same daily decisions that they would make for their own child. Every placement plan will be individual to the child and their circumstances.

As a foster carer, you are expected to undertake training which will help you care for the child. You also need to demonstrate how your care meets national training, support and development standards. These standards have been specially adapted for kinship foster carers and the fostering service should provide support to meet them.

Parents' rights and responsibilities

Who has parental responsibility depends on whether there is a court order in place and what that order is.

Speak to your social worker about how this might work in your situation and what rights you, the parents and children's services have.

When a child is accommodated under section 20 of the Children Act 1989 and placed with you as a kinship foster carer, the parents still have parental responsibility. Children's services work with the child's parents but cannot override their wishes. They will support with agreement of day-to-day arrangements and decision-making.

If children are being cared for as a result of a care order, parental responsibility is shared between the parents and the local authority.

Looked-after child (LAC) reviews can be used to make decisions about the child. They inform their care plan, which means carers, parents and professionals can all input.

Children's services will approve the arrangement

Children's services will assess and approve you as a foster carer. It is a thorough process, which usually takes several months to complete.

Children's services should provide you with information about the assessment process so that you know what is expected of you and how you will be assessed. This includes the criteria and the support to be offered to you during the assessment process.

The local authority will want to collect some information about you and your family before completing a full assessment. This is to see if there are any major obstacles to you becoming a foster carer. Sometimes they call this a 'viability assessment'.

If you offer to become a kinship foster carer, but children's services decide not to assess you, you can ask for their reasons in writing. If this happens, it may be helpful to get support from an organisation that can advise you on your legal rights: see chapter 15.

The fostering assessment process

The assessment to become a foster carer has 2 stages.

Stage 1 includes:

- gathering information about your family
- interviews with 2 referees
- a medical
- checking where you live

They will also check if you have a criminal record by doing an enhanced Disclosure and Barring Service (DBS) check on you and other members of your household. However, this will not necessarily prevent you from becoming a foster carer if the check does not include violent or sexual offences.

> A **Disclosure and Barring Service (DBS)** is a way for children's services to check details of any spent and unspent convictions, cautions, final warnings or reprimands. There are different types of DBS checks from basic to enhanced with a check of the barred lists.
>
> You, and any other household members over 18 (sometimes 16), would require an enhanced DBS check if you're considering becoming a kinship foster carer.

During the first stage, children's services can decide not to continue your assessment if they feel that you are not suitable. They must write to you to say why.

Stage 2 of the assessment will look at the qualities and skills you are likely to need to care for the child you want to foster. It takes into account standards set by the government.

The assessing social worker will get to know you, your experience and your family makeup. You will learn more about the role of a foster carer and how you will be supported.

The assessment can be useful in making sure that you are properly informed and prepared for your role as a foster carer.

When the assessment report is complete, it will be considered by a fostering panel. You will be able to read the report and attend the panel, and you can take someone to support you if you wish.

The fostering assessment process *continued*

The panel makes a recommendation about your approval to the fostering service's 'decision maker'. This will be a senior manager in children's services.

Looking after yourself

You might be surprised by how thorough the fostering assessment is. Kinship carers sometimes feel it is intrusive. The assessment will look into your history, your parenting experiences, and your mental and physical health. Sometimes, the process might bring up memories from your past that you find difficult to revisit.

Try to make sure that you give yourself space and have someone to talk to, to help you through the process.

Specific considerations for kinship foster carers

Guidance published by the Department for Education in 2024 outlines some specific considerations local authorities should make when assessing kinship foster carers.

The guidance confirms that:

- if kinship foster carers don't meet the national minimum standards for fostering, the fostering assessment panel should not make negative recommendations based only on this

- when a kinship foster carer is being assessed for approval for a specific child or children only, there is no need to consider their suitability to care for other children as with mainstream foster carers

You can read more in 'Kinship Care: Statutory guidance for local authorities' published by the Department for Education (pages 23-31) on **GOV.UK**.

If you are not approved after assessment

If the decision maker thinks that you should not be approved, they will send you something called a 'qualifying determination'.

You will be given 28 days to object or apply for a review of your application through independent review. This is called the independent review mechanism (IRM).

The IRM can review fostering applications and will make its own recommendation to the fostering service. The decision maker must take this into account.

If you are not approved, it is still possible that you could become a special guardian (see chapter 6). Speak to your social worker or get independent legal advice. Chapter 15 includes organisations that provide legal information and advice.

The placement plan sets out how long the arrangement lasts

How long the fostering placement is expected to last will depend on the child's circumstances. It could be just for a few weeks, or until the child turns 18.

The local authority can end the placement with you if they feel that it is no longer the most appropriate place for the child to live.

Before ending the placement of a looked-after child with a foster carer, the local authority must hold a case review and take account of your views.

A foster carer can end the arrangement at any point by giving 28 days' written notice.

If the arrangement came about with the consent of parents, they can ask for the child to be returned to them. But you should speak to a social worker from children's services before you return the child to the care of their parents. You can contact them during the day or at night on an out-of-hours number: ask your supervising social worker to give you these contact details. If you are concerned that the child is at immediate risk of harm, then call 999.

Applying for a legal order

If there are no plans for the child to return to the care of their parents, children's services may want you to apply for a legal order. The legal order would give you parental responsibility which is shared with the parents, and a long-term secure home for the child.

This may also be what you want. If one of these orders were granted this would mean that the child would no longer be in the care of children's services. Any care order would automatically come to an end.

Even if you agree that this is a positive step, you should not feel pushed into anything. Getting a child arrangements order or special guardianship order has implications for the support you would then be entitled to. This is likely to be less financial and practical support from children's services than if you were a kinship foster carer.

New guidance for local authorities published by the Department for Education in 2024 reaffirms that the fear of losing support should not become an obstacle to kinship carers taking over responsibility for the long-term care of a looked after child through applying for a child arrangements order or special guardianship order. However, the reality is that support beyond kinship foster care is largely discretionary, and you should talk to your local authority children's services to learn about how a change in legal order could affect the support you receive.

Before applying for an order, you should always seek legal advice (see chapter 15 for helpful organisations that can provide legal support). You should also clarify what support would be made available under any new arrangement and for how long. You can ask for this to be confirmed in writing.

For more information on your options and the process for legal orders, see chapter 5, child arrangements orders and chapter 6, special guardianship orders.

'Staying put' arrangements

If you are still fostering a young person when they turn 18 and you both decide to go on living together, then this is known as a 'staying put arrangement'.

Children's services should consider if this is an option when creating a pathway plan. The pathway plan is completed by the local authority to help young people prepare to leave care.

Staying put is not fostering. Children's services have a legal duty to support both you and the young person to go on living together. This support continues until they become 21, or they move out, whichever comes first.

Support for you must include financial support. This includes an allowance to cover all reasonable costs of supporting the young person to remain living with you.

Children's services should not set additional criteria to be met before support is given.

They can only refuse support in very exceptional circumstances, and if they consider that the staying put arrangement will not support the young person's welfare.

If the young person (aged 18 and over) moves out, and then returns to live with you before they turn 21, the local authority's staying put duties no longer apply. You can check with children's services to see if there is a time limit on moving out and returning to you, for example, if they are only away for a short time.

A social worker will provide support and supervision

Every foster carer is allocated a supervising social worker, whose job is to provide support and supervision.

The law requires approved foster carers to be reviewed at least every 12 months. You will be involved in this process, with feedback from the child you are caring for and from social workers included as well.

There are a number of independent organisations that can support you as a foster carer: see chapter 15 for a list.

The child's care plan and supervision

Every looked-after child has a care plan. This plan brings together everything that the foster carers and different professionals need to do for the child. You should be involved in drawing up the care plan and any reviews, and have a copy.

The child's social worker oversees how the plan is carried out. They must visit the child regularly to see that the placement is still meeting their needs. The frequency of visits varies, but is usually at least every 6 weeks. If the placement is due to last until the child is 18, visits will be every 3 months.

The child's social worker is responsible for managing the relationship between children's services and the child's parents. They should support you in any difficulties you may have with this.

They will also co-ordinate the provision of services to support the child and any therapeutic interventions provided by the local authority.

When they visit the child, their social worker should give you feedback. They should discuss how things are going with you and help you with any difficulties you are having.

Although their role is to focus on the child's needs, they should also provide support to you. They should help you to understand any difficulties the child has and how best to respond. It is often helpful to meet with your child's social worker as well as your supervising social worker to make sure you get the best support in caring for the child.

Looked-after child (LAC) reviews

One of your responsibilities as a kinship foster carer will be to attend looked-after child (LAC) reviews.

If the child is able to, they can decide if they want to be there, and who else they want to be there. The meetings will typically include you, the parents and any professionals involved in caring for the child, such as their social worker and teacher. It will be chaired by an independent reviewing officer (IRO). Parents don't have to attend in person (it is often not possible or safe).

LAC reviews are used to:

- review the child's care plan
- discuss the child's progress
- discuss the child's relationships, health, education, hobbies and interests
- make decisions and plans for the future

Independent reviewing officers (IROs)

Children's services have a duty to appoint an independent reviewing officer (IRO) for all children in their care.

The independent reviewing officer works for children's services. They work independently of the child's social worker. Their role is to review the care plan for the child.

Health assessments

A health assessment will be carried out for your child and will form part of their care plan. This is done to help the child access any physical or mental health care they might need. There will be an initial assessment then review health assessments. These are carried out by medical practitioners, nurses or midwives.

Personal Education Plan

Another part of the child's care plan is their Personal Education Plan (PEP). Your child's school will be involved in creating it. It includes:

- where the child requires support
- school history and their educational journey

- goals for academic achievement
- the child's views and aspirations

The plan ensures that looked-after children receive the necessary support to thrive academically and personally.

There is more information in chapter 11, supporting your kinship child at school.

You are eligible for support through fostering services

The social worker supervising you is your main source of information as a kinship foster carer. They are also your main link back to children's services.

They should make sure that you have all the information you need to provide appropriate care which meets the child's needs. They should provide advice and guidance about fostering.

Training for foster carers

Fostering services have a range of training available to help foster carers and you should have access to this. There may be additional training specifically to meet the needs of kinship foster carers. You could also be offered access to a support group that meets your needs as a kinship foster carer.

Fostering services should also provide support outside of office hours. Ask your supervising social worker for how to contact out-of-hours support in your area.

What you can expect from your local fostering service

Fostering services should meet a set of national minimum standards, set by the Department for Education. Search **GOV.UK** for 'Fostering services: national minimum standards'. Standard 30 describes the support which kinship foster carers should be given.

If you are kinship foster carer, it can be useful to know what it says and what you can expect from your local fostering service.

Other sources of help

There are a number of independent organisations that can support you as a foster carer: see chapter 15 under 'fostering' for a list.

Benefits and financial support

If you are a kinship foster carer, you are entitled to a foster care allowance to help you with the costs of caring for a child.

The amount you get depends on how many children you are fostering, their age, their needs, your experience and where you live. Minimum weekly allowances are set by the government each year and vary depending on the child's age and location. The minimum allowance is updated every April. For up-to-date minimum allowances, search **GOV.UK** for 'help and support for foster parents in England'.

For information on the foster care allowance, how you can claim, and what other benefits you can claim, see chapter 12 on benefits and financial support.

5. Child arrangements orders

Key points in this chapter:

- a child arrangements order is a legal order granted by the court, outlining the living situation of a child
- child arrangements orders have replaced contact and residence orders
- you have to meet certain criteria to be eligible to apply
- you share parental responsibility with the parents
- you will still need the parents' consent for a lot of decisions about the child
- you can apply online or ask a solicitor for help

What is a child arrangements order?

A child arrangements order (CAO), is a legal order made by the family court that states:

- where a child will live
- who a child can spend time with and for how long

A child arrangements order can state where a child will spend part of the week living with or having contact with a parent or other family member.

Child arrangements orders have replaced contact and residence orders. If you already have a residence order, you do not need to apply for a child arrangements order as both orders have the same effect.

Ann, Colin and their grandson

Ann and Colin have been bringing up their 4-year-old grandson Jon for the last 2 years, with the agreement of his mother.

Children's services have not been involved, but his mother's lifestyle involves heavy use of drugs and alcohol, and she's been in a succession of violent relationships.

Ann and Colin do not know where Jon's father (their son) is. They recently made a successful application to court for a child arrangements order to gain parental responsibility and to provide more stability for Jon.

Jon visits his mother regularly and Ann and Colin have a positive relationship with her.

Ann and Colin hope that Jon's mum will get the support she needs to get well, so Jon can one day return to her care.

Only certain people can apply for a child arrangements order

You can apply for a child arrangements order if you are:

- the child's grandparent, aunt, uncle, brother or sister (including by marriage or civil partnership), half-brother or half-sister, or step-parent, and they have lived with you for more than a year

- the child's appointed guardian following the death of a parent or special guardian

- a kinship foster carer and the child has lived with you for more than a year, or you have consent from everyone who has parental responsibility

- a private foster carer and the child has lived with you for at least 3 years

You can also apply for child arrangements order if you have consent from:

- everyone else who holds parental responsibility

- children's services, if the child is in their care

- anyone who already has a residence order or child arrangements order for the child

You must be 18 or over to apply. You cannot normally apply for a child aged 16 and over.

If you don't meet the criteria listed here, you can still apply to the family court for permission to apply.

You can apply online or ask a solicitor to help

You can apply for a child arrangements order online: search **GOV.UK** for 'child arrangements order'.

You can also get help from a solicitor. It is recommended that you get legal advice and support, and you may be eligible for legal aid.

You might be asked to attend a Mediation, Information and Assessment Meeting (MIAM). If you or the parent are eligible for legal aid you will both qualify for a free MIAM.

If neither of you are eligible for legal aid, you will have to pay for the MIAM. This is around £120 per person but can vary and changes every year.

Speaking to a mediator can help everyone agree on the care arrangements before you apply for a child arrangements order.

Support through legal aid

You may be eligible for support through legal aid, if you are applying for the order to protect a child who has been subject to or is at risk of abuse. It will depend on your financial circumstances and whether your case stands a reasonable chance of success.

Read chapter 14 on the legal process for more information about legal advice. Refer to chapter 15 for information on organisations that can provide legal information and advice.

Your rights and responsibilities

You share parental responsibility with the child's parents until they are 18 years old, unless the family court states otherwise.

You will need to make basic day-to-day decisions about the child, but would need to consult others with parental responsibility over major decisions such as:

- medical treatment (except in an emergency where the hospital will make a decision on the best course of treatment)
- schooling
- foreign travel
- hair cuts

You can take the child out of the country for up to 1 month but would need the permission of everyone else with parental responsibility for longer periods. If someone who has parental responsibility does not agree with your decisions, they can apply to the court for an order to stop you.

To clarify which decisions you can make, you might find it helpful to draw up a document which you and others with parental responsibility sign. If you have trouble arranging this with the parents, you can ask children's services for support. You can also ask Kinship for advice. See chapter 8 for more information on decision-making for the child in your care.

There are key differences between the rights you have with a child arrangements order and a special guardianship order (chapter 6). If you hold a special guardianship order you are able to make more decisions without the parents' input or consent.

If you and the child's parents cannot agree over particular issues, you can apply for a court order and the judge will make a decision.

Specific issue orders

A specific issue order (SIO) is a court order that decides a particular question about a child's upbringing. For example, which school a child should go to if the people with parental responsibility cannot agree. You are legally required to attend a MIAM (Mediation Information and Assessment Meeting) before applying for a SIO via the government's C100 form (available on the **GOV.UK** website).

Prohibited steps orders

A prohibited steps order (PSO) is a court order. It specifies particular things that someone with parental responsibility cannot legally do without the consent of another person with parental responsibility or the court. For example, it can prevent contact with someone who is regarded as a safeguarding risk to the child, or prevent someone with parental responsibility from relocating with the child to another country. You are legally required to attend a MIAM (Mediation Information and Assessment Meeting) before applying for a PSO via the government's C100 form (available on the **GOV.UK** website).

Parents retain parental responsibility

Parents share parental responsibility with you. They must be consulted over major decisions for the child.

They remain responsible for supporting the child financially, although in practice some can't or don't want to. If the parents are working, you can apply for financial support via Child Maintenance (see chapter 12 on benefits and financial support for more details).

The court approves the arrangements

When deciding, the court must make the child's welfare its main consideration.

It must follow the 'welfare checklist' by taking into consideration the following points:

- the child's wishes and feelings
- the child's physical, emotional and/or educational needs
- the likely effect on the child of any change in circumstances
- the child's age, sex, background and characteristics
- any harm which the child has suffered or is at risk of suffering
- how capable the parents, and any other person, are of meeting the child's needs
- the power of the court to make any other orders

The court will usually ask for a welfare report to be prepared by someone from the Children and Family Court Advisory and Support Service (Cafcass) or by children's services if they have been involved with the child.

Child arrangements orders last until the child is 18

If a care order (or interim care order) is made for the child by the local authority, this would bring the child arrangements order to an end. A parent can also apply to court to end an order.

There is no supervision or review of a child arrangements order after it has been granted.

'Staying put' arrangements, where a child remains with their carer when they turn 18, do not apply if you have a child arrangements order or a residence order, even if you previously fostered the young person. They may, however, be eligible for leaving care services. Check with your local children's services.

Support available

If children's services assess the child as being 'in need' they may provide family support services. This could include the cost of legal fees in connection with obtaining a child arrangements order, if they agree this is the best outcome for the child.

From September 2024 kinship carers with a child arrangements order, where the child was not previously looked after, will also be able to get information and advice from their virtual school. See chapter 11 supporting your kinship child at school for more information.

Benefits and financial support

There is a discretionary, means-tested child arrangements order allowance. You are more likely to get an allowance if the child was in care of children's services before the order was made. You should be able to read information about child arrangements order allowances in your local authority's kinship local offer. You can challenge the local authority if you're refused financial support. See chapter 13 on working with your local authority for information on how to make a complaint.

You may be able to access other benefits, for example benefits for families. This could include Child Benefit, the child element in Universal Credit if you're of working age or Pension Credit if you're of pension age. It can also include the adoption and special guardianship support fund.

For information on what financial benefits and support you might be entitled to and the support mentioned here, see chapter 12.

Find your virtual school, kinship local offer and other local information, services and support on our postcode search tool, Kinship Compass: **kinship.org.uk/in-your-area**

Notes

6. Special guardianship orders

Key points in this chapter:

- a special guardianship order is a legal order granted by the court, designed to give a child a permanent home

- a special guardianship order may be part of care proceedings, where a child is moving from the care of children's services

- the child must usually have lived with you for at least a year before you apply to the court for an order, but even if they haven't you can still apply to court for permission to seek an order

- you must notify the local authority 3 months before you apply for an order, and they will prepare a report

- the order is intended to be permanent and lasts until the child is 18

- you share parental responsibility with the child's parents but can exercise this without taking account of their views

- you should be assessed for support services available from your local authority

- you might be entitled to receive a special guardianship allowance, although this will be means-tested and reviewed regularly

What is a special guardianship order?

A special guardianship order (SGO) is an order made by the family court. It is designed to give a child who cannot live with their parents a permanent home with someone who knows them. The person or people named on the special guardianship order will become the child's special guardian.

As a special guardian, you have parental responsibility for the child until they are 18 years old. The child will live with you permanently.

You will make both day-to-day decisions about their care and more important decisions about their life. While you can overrule the parents, you are encouraged to work with them if possible.

If the child you are caring for is in the care of children's services, your local authority may encourage you to apply for a special guardianship order.

However, it is important to know that once the order is granted, the child would no longer be in the care of children's services, and any support that has been provided under a different arrangement may stop. Any support going forward will be outlined in the support plan.

Mary and her grandchildren

Mary was asked by her local children's services department to take on the care of her 5 grandchildren aged 2, 3, 5, 9 and 12. The children were in the care of children's services. Mary became the children's kinship foster carer, and received an allowance to help her support the children.

Children's services suggested as part of their care plan that Mary apply for a special guardianship order to give the children stability and permanence. Mary agreed, but was concerned that she would not be eligible for foster care allowance once the order was granted.

After Mary raised this concern, children's services agreed as part of the children's support plan that Mary would continue to receive an allowance until the children reached 18 to make sure she could meet the children's needs. This meant that Mary was able to become her grandchildren's special guardian without the concern that financial support would stop.

Please note: every local authority is different and the support you can get will vary. Speak to your local authority and seek legal advice to ensure you get the best support possible for you and your family.

Arrangements are often made through children's services but can also be made privately

If children's services are involved in your arrangement, then you will go through **public law proceedings**. Ask children's services what the process will involve and what you will need to do.

If children's services were not involved in placing the child with you, and you and the parent decides that special guardianship would be in the best interests of the child, you will go through **private law proceedings**. This is an arrangement between individuals, such as family members.

You need to tell children's services in writing 3 months before the date you want to apply to the court for a special guardianship order.

For information on the process of becoming a special guardian, see gov.uk/apply-special-guardian.

> **Before you apply for a special guardianship order, whether children's services are involved or not, it's important that you get legal advice. Chapter 14 of this guide has some further information about finding legal advice, getting legal aid and what to expect from the legal process.**

At the end of this chapter, there is space for you to make notes on the process you need to follow for your local children's services, and/or following advice from your solicitor.

Only certain people are eligible to apply for a special guardianship order

You have the right to apply to the family court for a special guardianship order if:

- you already have a residence order or child arrangements order for the child

- you are the child's grandparent, aunt, uncle, brother or sister (including by half blood, marriage or civil partnership) or step-parent, and the child has lived with you for at least a year

- you are a guardian of the child who was appointed by the parent or special guardian to look after the child following their death

- the child is in the care of children's services, and they consent to you making an application

- you are a local authority foster carer who has had the child placed with you for at least a year, or

- the child has been living with you for at least 3 years out of the last 5

You can also apply if you have the consent of:

- children's services, if the child is in their care, or

- everyone else who holds parental responsibility, including anyone who already holds a residence or child arrangements order

If you're not covered by any of the above circumstances, you can still make an application to the court for permission to apply.

You must be 18 or over to apply for a special guardianship order.

Special guardianship assessment process

A social worker will complete an assessment to show that you are able to care for the child. The assessment goes into a lot of detail and includes information about you and your background, the child and any support you think you will need.

The process should be done over 5-8 visits and will cover a wide range of topics. As well as having an enhanced Disclosure and Barring Service (DBS) check and giving employment and relationship histories, you'll be asked about how you were parented, and family relationships. It doesn't matter if you've had difficult experiences in the past, but the social worker will be interested in how you dealt with them.

> A **Disclosure and Barring Service (DBS)** is a way for children's services to check details of any spent and unspent convictions, cautions, final warnings or reprimands. There are different types of DBS checks from basic to enhanced with a check of the barred lists.
>
> You, and any other household members over 18 (sometimes 16), would require an enhanced DBS check if you're considering becoming a special guardian.

You may be talking about upsetting topics, so it's a good idea to plan with the social worker when these visits happen, so that you have time to wind down and have a break afterwards. It's important to get support, and ask your social worker for help getting support if you need to. More information about support for you is available in chapter 8, becoming a kinship carer.

Towards the end of the process you should be given a draft copy of the assessment and asked if you think it is an accurate assessment.

If the outcome of the assessment is negative, you can respond in writing, challenging the reasons for the negative assessment. This will go to the court to make a decision. If they agree with your challenge they may order a new assessment.

The court will decide whether to grant the special guardianship order. See chapter 14 for further details of the court process.

Once the order is granted, if the child is looked-after by a different local authority, notify them. Otherwise, notify the local authority where you live.

Special guardianship support plan

A key part of the special guardianship process will be creating a support plan. Children's services create the plan but you can input into it. It acts as a planning tool that can be used after the initial assessment and planning process to set out the support provided to you, the child and their family.

The support plan is crucial to getting the support you need as a special guardian. It is an important document. It should be specific to the child and set out clearly the support that will be made available to ensure their needs are met.

You may want to ask a solicitor to advise you on what is included in the plan. See chapter 14 for how to get legal advice. The judge should review your support plan.

The plan should be reviewed on a yearly basis, or whenever there are significant changes or transition points (e.g. moving to a new house, transferring from primary to secondary school).

There is a checklist at the end of this chapter with key things to discuss about your support plan.

Fostering and special guardianship orders

If you are fostering a child, children's services should not pressure you to agree to apply for parental responsibility, such as through a special guardianship order.

Special guardianship provides more security for the child. With parental responsibility, you have all the rights of a parent and the child cannot be removed by children's services or anyone else without going through child protection and court processes.

As a family you need to weigh up whether you want independence from children's services but potentially less support.

Your rights and responsibilities

As a special guardian, you have parental responsibility for the child until they are 18 years old. The child will live with you permanently. You will make both day-to-day decisions about their care and more important decisions about their life.

Unless it is unsafe or difficult to do so, working with parents on decision-making can work in the best interests of the child. Keep parents informed about decisions, and get their consent for important decisions including:

- changing the child's surname
- changing the child's religion
- taking the child abroad for more than 3 months
- putting the child up for adoption
- surgery that doesn't improve the child's health, such as circumcision

If you cannot get consent, you can ask the court to decide by completing a C2 form. This form is to make an application in existing court proceedings. You can find it by searching 'C2 form' on **GOV.UK**.

If someone else who has parental responsibility does not agree with your decisions about the child they can ask the court for permission to make an application for an order, but the court does not have to agree to grant permission.

Parents retain parental responsibility and share this with the holder(s) of the special guardianship order. However, special guardians have overriding parental responsibility.

If it is safe and feasible to do so, it can be helpful to write up an agreement between you and the parents that lists some of the decisions you might need to make, and who will be involved in making them. See chapter 8 for further information.

Parents' rights and responsibilities

Parents retain parental responsibility and share this with the holder(s) of the special guardianship order. As a special guardian you have overriding parental responsibility but you should not feel you have to exclude parents from all decision-making if it is safe and feasible to include them.

Parents remain financially responsible for a child who is subject to a special guardianship order, although in practice the responsibility may fall on the special guardian.

If parents want to challenge your responsibility and want to resume care of the child, they first must ask permission of the court to make an application. They need to demonstrate that they have changed their lives sufficiently to be able to make an application. They also need to demonstrate why a change of circumstances would be beneficial to the child.

The arrangement lasts until the child is 18

The purpose of special guardianship is to provide the child with stability for the long term. It can only be ended by asking the court for an application to end the order.

'Staying put' arrangements, where you can get support for a child to remain with you when they turn 18, do not apply if you have a special guardianship order, even if you previously fostered the young person. Children can continue living with you once they're over 18 if they choose to.

No one will supervise or review the order

There is no supervision or review of a special guardianship order once it is granted.

You are entitled to support from children's services

Children's services must provide support services for special guardians and the children in their care in their local area, which may include:

- help with contact arrangements
- therapy
- counselling
- advice and information
- access to support groups
- respite
- financial support
- training courses

Ask children's services about an assessment for support. Or speak to your solicitor, if you have one, about what you might be entitled to.

All children's services departments should have adetails of their kinship local offer (previously known as a family and friends care policy).

Find your local authority's kinship local offer (previously family and friends care policy) and other local information, services and support on our postcode search tool, Kinship Compass: **kinship.org.uk/in-your-area**

Financial support for special guardians

As a special guardian, you may be able to get financial help from children's services, such as a special guardianship allowance. Children's services will assess your financial situation, decide what support you should get and review it every year.

You are more likely to be paid an allowance if the child was previously placed with you as a kinship foster carer (looked-after child). You may not receive the same level of payments that you did as a kinship foster carer, because allowances are means-tested.

Any allowance you do get should be the same or more than the minimum fostering allowance rates set by the government before taking your financial situation into account.

The financial support you can get depends on where you live and the age of the child you are caring for. The support available should be detailed in your children's services kinship local offer.

Review of financial support

If there is a change in your circumstances, you can request a review at any time. The regulations state, that if the child was looked after by children's services before the special guardianship order was made, children's services must carry out an assessment for support services. But if the child was not looked after by children's services, they may do an assessment, but they are not required to.

You may also be entitled to:

- apply to support from the adoption and special guardianship support fund
- one-off payments for a child in need, see section 17 support in chapter 12

For information on what financial benefits and support you might be entitled to as a special guardian, see chapter 12.

What happens if you and the child move to a different area?

If the child was looked after by the local authority before the special guardianship order was made

The children's services department that was responsible for the child before the order was made is responsible for providing non-financial support services for up to 3 years.

- this responsibility continues even if the child moves to a new local authority area
- after 3 years, responsibility passes to the local authority area where the child now lives

Financial support agreed before the special guardianship order was made remains the responsibility of the original local authority children's services department.

- this support will continue for as long as was agreed in your support plan
- if there is a change in your circumstances, such as an increase in income, the support may be adjusted or stopped following an annual review

If the child was not looked after before the special guardianship order was made

The local authority area where the child lives will be responsible for all special guardianship support.

Therefore, if the child moves, the new local authority area will be responsible for all support, including financial support.

The Children Act 1989 and the Special Guardianship Regulations 2005 outline these responsibilities. However, disputes may arise between children's services departments over which one is responsible.

Judges in the family court have stated that:

- it is up to the local authorities to resolve responsibility issues between themselves
- special guardians should not be left without support while authorities determine which one is responsible

If you need to make a complaint to the local authorities involved, refer to chapter 13 on working with your local authority for further information.

Special guardianship support plan checklist

The social worker putting together your support plan may be using a template so it's important that you ask for what you would like included. Think about what you might need in the future, as well as now. It can include:

- financial support – one-off payments and ongoing allowances
- support around contact with parents, including supervised contact or contact in a contact centre if necessary
- help to obtain suitable accommodation
- support for childcare
- support for the child after reaching 18, especially if they are moving into their own home or staying in education
- specialist help, for example:
  - bereavement counselling
  - support with behaviour
  - parenting programmes
  - respite
  - therapeutic work
  - assessment for diagnoses of special educational needs and disability, for example: ADHD, or autism if necessary

My checklist for applying for special guardianship

We've left this space for you to create your own checklist.

7. Adoption

Key points in this chapter:

- adoption is a permanent arrangement which transfers all parental responsibility to the adopters

- in almost all cases, it is not appropriate for kinship carers to adopt the child they care for, instead a special guardianship is the best option for a safe, secure permanent home (see chapter 6)

What is adoption?

Adoption is the process where a child becomes a legal and permanent member of a new family. An adoption order ends the child's legal ties with their family. All rights and responsibilities move to the adoptive parents, who will make decisions about the child and who they have contact with.

In almost all cases, it is not appropriate for kinship carers to adopt the child they care for. Instead, the family court will usually consider a special guardianship order or child arrangements order to make sure the child has a safe, secure place to live.

Melanie and her nephew

Melanie took on the care of her nephew Simon when he was just 6 months old, following the death of both parents in a car accident.

Melanie was just 18 at the time and initially received support and financial help from her own parents, but she began to worry about Simon's future. As soon as she was 21 she applied to adopt Simon.

A social worker investigated the circumstances on behalf of the court. They recommended that Simon should be adopted by Melanie as he had been brought up by her from such a young age. The court granted an adoption order.

Only certain people can apply to adopt a child

You can apply to adopt a child if they have lived with you for at least 3 of the last 5 years and you are the child's:

- grandparent
- aunt or uncle
- step-parent
- brother or sister
- half-brother or half-sister through marriage or civil partnership

You must write to your local authority's children's services department to tell them you want to apply for an adoption order at least 3 months before you make the application. A social worker will need to prepare a report for the court.

If you are a kinship foster carer, you can apply to adopt a child who has lived with you for at least a year. You must also have consent from the child's parents or get approval from the family court to adopt without their consent.

If you are thinking of adopting a child who is placed with you as a local authority foster carer this must be consistent with their care plan. You should discuss this carefully with the social worker, and never feel under pressure to adopt without considering the consequences of taking on parental responsibility.

You must be 21 or over to apply for an adoption order.

Your rights and responsibilities

Once you adopt a child you legally become their parent(s) in every respect. You can exercise parental responsibility in the same way as any other parent would.

Parents' rights and responsibilities

An adoption order completely breaks the link between the child and their parents. Parental responsibility transfers completely and permanently to the adopters.

However, many adoptions are 'open' in that the child – and sometimes the adopters – remain in regular contact with the parents.

The court approves adoption orders

You must give children's services where you live written notice that you intend to apply for an adoption order. A social worker will then prepare a report for the court. For more detail on the adoption process, see **gov.uk/child-adoption**.

Adoptions are not supervised or reviewed. A social worker will be responsible for ensuring that the child's welfare is met from the time you give notice that you are going to apply to adopt until the order is granted.

Adoption is a permanent, lifelong arrangement

An adoption order cannot be revoked.

You are eligible for specialist support

Your local authority's children's services department must provide a range of support for people affected by adoption. You can ask for an assessment to find out if you are able to access these support services.

Benefits and financial support

For information on what financial benefits and support you might be entitled to, see chapter 12.

For further information related to adoption, find details in chapter 15 on how to contact Adoption UK or Adoption England.

Notes

8. Becoming a kinship carer: things to consider

"

It was really useful to me to know that other kinship carers were experiencing the same issues, that it wasn't just something that I was doing wrong.

Kinship carer

Kinship carers often say the rewards of caring are enormous. Becoming a kinship carer can be life changing, but the experience of being a kinship carer can bring significantly more pressures to day-to-day family life.

This chapter covers:
- making decisions for your child
- managing your work life
- the impact on relationships
- managing difficult circumstances
- preparing financially
- preparing your home or finding new accommodation

Contact Kinship's advice line

You can call us for free on **0300 123 7015**

For more information, including our opening hours visit **kinship.org.uk/advice-line**

This chapter looks at some of the most common practical and emotional challenges that kinship carers face and where to get support and advice. Everyone's situation is different. You might have additional challenges, but you are not alone.

Your local authority has a duty to provide family support services to promote the upbringing of children in kinship care. You can find out more information about this in the relevant chapters on different types of kinship care (chapters 2-7). However, kinship carers tell us they often find it difficult to get the support they need from their local authority. You can read more about working with your local authority children's services and the support they should be providing you in chapter 13.

You can get support from Kinship through our services, including our website and advice line, local peer support groups and programme of training and workshops. For more information on other helpful organisations that can provide support, see chapter 15.

Deciding if this is right for you

People become kinship carers in different ways for different reasons. In many communities, raising children within their wider family is normal. For some carers a crisis leads to the arrangement.

Whatever the circumstance, your feelings matter. You might have thought very carefully about becoming a kinship carer, or everything may have happened in a big rush. You may have lots of complicated emotions, such as feeling responsible, angry, or that you have no real choice but to help.

None of these feelings are wrong, but if you are clear about why you are offering to help it will enable you to make better informed decisions. Caring full-time for a child is a huge undertaking and will be life changing. People often need help to think about and talk through the implications. Specialist, independent legal advice is essential if the plan for the child's care involves a formal arrangement.

You can still say no if you have weighed it all up and feel this isn't the right choice. Only you know the right decision for you. If you feel it's not the right decision, talk to whoever has parental responsibility, to children's services, explore a family group conference or other meeting where family-led decision-making takes place.

A **family group conference** is a decision-making meeting of family members to help them to make plans for a child's care and protection. For more information about family group decision making see chapter 13 on working with your local authority children's services.

Practical considerations

Making decisions for the child in your care

What decisions you can make for the child depends on the type of kinship carer you are.

Depending on who has parental responsibility, the child's parents may still be fully responsible and able to make all decisions relating to the child. This can be tricky to navigate.

Decisions can be seen as 'big' or 'small', and which ones you can make depends on your specific kinship care arrangement.

'Small' decisions could be:

- what to eat for dinner
- how someone is dressed
- sleepovers

'Big' decisions could be:

- where to go to school
- haircuts
- hospital treatments and medication

If it is safe and feasible to do so, it can be helpful to write up an agreement between you and the parents that lists some of the decisions you might need to make, and who will be involved in making them. This can be an informal agreement, but if there are really important decisions expected you may want these included as part of a formal or legal agreement. If you or the child have a social worker, you can ask them for support communicating with family members.

Your agreement might include:

- what rules you'll agree to (such as bedtimes, when homework is done, staying out late)
- what you'll do in emergencies
- how you'll approach big decisions, such as choosing a secondary school
- how you'll talk to children about the situation and what you tell them
- how you'll communicate and resolve any disagreements

Your life and interests

"I feel my grandchild misses out on activities because I have to work. I also feel I miss out on training courses that would be beneficial to her upbringing. I do consider us lucky as I realise things could be so much worse than they are. We have our health which is so important."
Kinship carer

You might be retired, still studying, unable to work due to health, or be at the height of your career. You might have children, or not. Whatever your situation, your life will change significantly when you take on a kinship child, and kinship carers can find this very difficult. You might have complicated feelings about the sacrifices you will need to make to take care of the child.

Do you have other caring responsibilities to fit in? Consider who might be able to help you with any childcare you need. Talk these issues through with someone you trust and who can help you think clearly. This is a huge decision, and you may feel overwhelmed.

See chapter 15 for a list of helpful organisations who can provide emotional wellbeing and mental health support.

Managing work and childcare

If you are working, one of the big considerations of kinship care is managing work and your new childcare responsibilities. You can read about help with childcare costs in chapter 12.

Flexible working

If you are employed you can request a flexible working arrangement, however long you have worked there. This might include working part-time or as a job share. It could be working longer hours over fewer days or working from home. Employers must deal with requests in a 'reasonable manner'.

For more information see **gov.uk/flexible-working**.

Unpaid parental leave

If you have been with your employer for more than a year, you may be entitled to up to 18 weeks unpaid parental leave for each child you are caring for. You can take a maximum of 4 weeks in one year for each qualifying child.

This only applies if you have parental responsibility or are applying for a legal order that will grant you parental responsibility for a child aged under 18. You are not eligible if you are a foster carer.

For more information see **gov.uk/parental-leave**.

Kinship Friendly Employer scheme

Ask if your organisation is a Kinship Friendly Employer. If not, encourage them to become one.

Many companies have family friendly policies like flexible working and paid parental leave which don't cover kinship carers. But you can ask them to. Kinship carers have been successful in approaching their employers, explaining their situation and gaining support from them.

Kinship provides a free framework and toolkit to help any employer – from any sector and of any size to introduce kinship friendly policies.

For more information search for 'Kinship friendly employer' on the Kinship website.

Emotional considerations

Challenging circumstances

One of the biggest challenges is that kinship care arrangements can happen in an unplanned way and at a time of family crisis.

You might be taking on children late at night because their parent has been admitted to hospital, or a social worker might have asked you to care for the children because they are considered at risk if left at home.

> *"Her mum came back for a month, relapsed in that month and then had a major relapse at the beginning of November that year and I literally went and took the child. I just took her and rang social services"*
> Kinship carer

Starting family life in this way can leave both you and the child feeling shocked and unprepared.

Some children may have suffered abuse and neglect. Caring for children who have endured childhood adversity can be very difficult both emotionally and physically. Children may need different types of parenting and support to overcome traumatic experiences.

Coming to terms and living with the consequences of harm caused to children by your family members or friends can be difficult to accept. It's normal to feel angry or sad.

It is important to recognise that you are doing your best in a challenging situation, and to seek support when you can.

What you can do

You can get help from specialist organisations on a range of circumstances including addiction, abuse and trauma: see chapter 15 for a list of helpful organisations.

Strain on family relationships

Although there are enormous benefits to a child remaining within their family network, taking on a child in such difficult circumstances can affect the whole family.

As the kinship carer you might feel very disappointed and angry towards parents, feeling they have let down their own children. You might also be realising that things have been kept from you, such as abuse or addiction.

Parents might feel resentful of the kinship carer. They may not understand why they cannot care for their own children, and sometimes may try to undermine the arrangements that have been put in place.

Children might not understand why they are unable to live with their parents and can get caught in the middle of difficulties between the adults. Sometimes children may blame their kinship carers.

Your own family, if you have a partner or your own children, are likely to be affected too. You may find that not everyone agrees with the situation.

The strain on family relationships can be difficult. It is important to put the child's needs first, but it's not always easy to do this.

What you can do

- see chapter 10 for more on managing arrangements with parents

- if you're working with your local authority, children's services or a social worker, then asking for a family group conference can help to communicate arrangements across the family (see chapter 13 for more information)

- family mediation can help if you are having difficulties resolving issues: the Family Mediation Council provides details of local mediators: **familymediationcouncil.org.uk**

Financial support

Navigating the unexpected cost of raising a child, while trying to establish what additional support you might be entitled to, is one of the most complex challenges kinship carers face.

Taking on children can mean you need to make some major changes. You may be retired and living on a pension. You may be employed or still in education and feel that you have to give up your job or your studies to care for the children. Either way, you may have to make some big decisions which could affect your finances.

What you can do

There may be financial support available. What you get depends on your particular arrangement. This is detailed in the chapters on kinship care arrangements (chapters 2-7) and more detail on benefits and financial support in chapter 12.

Housing and accommodation

Lack of suitable accommodation is another challenge often faced by kinship carers, especially if you already have children living in the home.

Living in cramped conditions may be manageable for a short period, but it can easily add to the pressures of caring for a child.

What you can do

If you live in social housing, housing departments should recognise your needs as a kinship carer. Where possible you should be given priority to move to more suitable accommodation if this will prevent the need for a child to be taken into the care of children's services.

Local authorities have the power to give financial assistance towards housing costs where they assess this as the most appropriate way to safeguard and promote a child's welfare. Although given limited resources this power is likely to be used only in exceptional circumstances.

Quick reference guide

Issue	Who can help you/who to contact
Needs of the child or children you are going to care for	<ul><li>your local authority and children's services</li><li>health visitor</li><li>the child's social worker</li><li>SEND (special educational needs and disability) provision at school</li><li>virtual school head (see chapter 11 for more information)</li></ul>
Who has parental responsibility and your legal position This can affect what decisions you can and can't make	<ul><li>your local authority and children's services</li><li>a social worker (if you have one)</li><li>organisations that provide legal support (see chapter 15 for a list)</li></ul>
Contact with parents This can be challenging as you establish a routine for the child to meet with their parents See chapter 10, managing contact and family relationships.	<ul><li>your local authority and children's services</li><li>a social worker (if you have one)</li><li>the child's parents</li><li>the child's wider family network depending on the relationship and your situation</li><li>Kinship's advice line and peer support groups</li><li>the police – contact them immediately if you feel that you or the child are at risk of physical harm</li></ul>
Education You might worry about your child's education and the support available to them. See chapter 11, supporting your kinship child at school.	<ul><li>the child's school (teachers, headteacher, designated teacher, SENCo - special educational needs coordinator)</li><li>the parent teacher association (PTA)</li><li>school governors</li><li>virtual school or virtual school headteacher (see chapter 11)</li><li>a social worker (if you have one)</li></ul>
Finances You'll need to think about what it might cost to provide for any child you are caring for and whether you can manage this without financial help	<ul><li>your local authority and children's services</li><li>the parents, if this is feasible/appropriate</li><li>your solicitor about what financial support might be available</li><li>additional financial support (see chapter 12)</li></ul>
Housing and accommodation You might worry you don't have enough space or furniture.	<ul><li>your local authority and children's services – they may be able to provide additional help</li><li>your council or housing provider</li><li>your mortgage provider (if applicable)</li><li>additional financial support (see chapter 12)</li></ul>
Your job Think about how you will balance your job and caring responsibilities	<ul><li>ask your employer for flexible working arrangements and carer's leave</li><li>additional financial support (see chapter 12)</li></ul>

Issue	Who can help you/who to contact
Practical support for you Think how you might ask for practical help	• friends and family • neighbours • peer support groups (see chapter 15) • local authority/children's services for children with additional needs • community organisations, local and national charities, faith groups
Emotional support for you Think about how you can take care of your emotional needs	• family and friends • Kinship's peer support groups or 'Someone Like Me' service (see chapter 15) • Kinship's programme of training and workshops (see chapter 15) • parent mental health support organisations (see chapter 15) • NHS Services or your GP

Next steps

- if you're working with children's services or a social worker, ask them what support is available to you

- read through chapter 15, helpful organisations, to see which organisations can help with the challenges you are facing

- visit **kinship.org.uk** to explore support available such as the advice line, programme of training and workshops, 'Someone Like Me', and peer support groups

Contact Kinship's advice line

You can call us for free on **0300 123 7015**

For more information, including our opening hours visit **kinship.org.uk/advice-line**

9. Emotional support for your kinship child

"

Supporting her through this difficult journey, witnessing tears into smiles, enabling her to embrace opportunities and contentment to go forward into her adult life, is amazing.

Kinship carer

This chapter covers:

- how to talk to the child in your care about the situation
- some of the behaviours that are common in kinship children
- trauma, attachment and other emotional support and mental health needs
- tools to help you best support your child's mental wellbeing

Helping the child settle into your care

There is a good chance you will already know the child well before you become their kinship carer, but this isn't always the case. Whatever the situation, make some extra time to talk with them. Make sure they know they can ask any questions and say how they are feeling.

Talk to the child about what is happening and find a way to explain in a way that matches their understanding. Reassure them that they are loved and cared for.

Be open and listen to their worries. The child may be thinking about how they will bring their clothes and toys, and about staying in contact with their siblings.

You can also speak to those who have been caring for them to learn more about the things they like doing and their day-to-day routines. Ask about contact information for school friends, activities they attend, meals they like to eat and medication they take.

Explaining the situation to children

Explaining to the child the need for them to be in your care will depend on their age and the situation. Some children may not understand what is happening, or why they cannot live with their parents. Some parents may not want to tell their children the full story of why they cannot continue to care for them. It may fall to you to figure out how best to share the answers to the many questions they may have.

If possible, it can be useful to speak with the parents about what you'll share with the child. If a social worker is supporting you, they may be able to advise what is appropriate to share, depending on the child's age. School and the child's teachers could also be a helpful source of support.

Some children may have lots of questions. Try to answer honestly where you can and if it is appropriate. Others may be worrying and thinking about it, but not asking any questions at all. Try to create ways in which the child coming into your care can express themselves.

Most importantly, reassure the child that the situation is not their fault, and that they are loved and cared for. You may need to repeat this, often.

Creating a family story

Children in kinship care may need extra support to make sense of their experiences and feel part of a family. If there has been a lot of disruption, children can feel confused about their lives.

As a kinship carer you may not have all the information about your child's experiences. You might not know when your child first walked or their first word. There can be a lot of sadness about the missing pieces.

Kinship children benefit from having a family story that supports them and their identity. You can help them to create their own story.

Sharing experiences and open communication

Talking, listening and playing together, at the child's pace, is a good place to start. This will open up communication between you and your child.

Exploring and creating memories

Looking at past photographs and then taking photographs together can help you create connection. Connection can help your child understand themselves, feel part of a family and navigate the outside world.

Positive stories from kinship families

Finding positive stories about other kinship families can be useful. Your child and you can see yourselves reflected in the lives of others and this can be helpful in building a strong family identity. People working with kinship carers have found using Paddington Bear (raised by his aunt) a great positive talking point with young children.

It can be hard to talk about past experiences, and you might be worried about getting it wrong. Ask for help if you need it.

Life story work

Life story work is a way of sensitively talking through and processing a child or young person's difficult experiences. It is often a relief for the child to have those experiences acknowledged, and to have support to understand them.

The aim of life story work is to share ideas, feelings and information that help the child to understand their past experiences. This includes why they were unable to live with their parents and, if applicable, why social workers came into their life.

Life story work usually involves a finished product, such as a book. But for children, understanding their story is a process: it won't happen in one session. Life story work should support a child's emotional wellbeing and future understanding of their situation. Sometimes kinship carers create their own book which they and the child can build on in the future.

If you are working with a social worker, you can ask them about getting support with life story work for your child. They can support you in having difficult conversations, and help children process their experiences.

Kathy, Phillip and their nephew Freddy

Kathy and Phillip became kinship carers to Kathy's nephew, Freddy, when he was a toddler. Freddy came into their care because Freddy had suffered serious abuse by his father, Kathy's brother. Growing up, Kathy and Phillip didn't ever mention Freddy's father, and Freddy didn't seem to remember him.

Over time, as Freddy grew older, they realised that Freddy didn't know that Kathy was his dad's sister, or that Kathy was related to him at all. They knew they needed to tell Freddy, but didn't know how to go about doing that.

Kathy and Phillip reached out to a social worker. Over a period of 6 months, they worked with the whole family to very carefully introduce Freddy to the fact that Kathy and Phillip were his aunt and uncle. Kathy and Phillip felt a huge sense of relief and the family were stronger as a result.

Emotional issues, poor mental health or behavioural challenges in kinship children

It is common for children in kinship care to show symptoms of emotional issues or poor mental health.

Children in kinship care have often experienced events in their early life that show up as behaviours or symptoms in the present. These could include:

- trouble sleeping
- tantrums (a result of not knowing how to manage big emotions) and meltdowns (being overwhelmed)
- physical threats and aggression
- trouble socialising or making friends
- low mood or mood swings
- difficulty communicating
- refusing to go to school
- fear of being alone
- struggling to go to the toilet, or going more often
- regressing back to much younger behaviours
- finding transitions tricky: regularly disruptive or upset when changing surroundings or activities (such as getting dressed or at bedtimes)

These symptoms and behaviours may be hard for you to manage and can feel personal. It is important to remember that all behaviour is communication. Understanding how trauma has affected your child is the first step to dealing positively with their emotions and behaviours.

Mental health and special educational needs (SEN)

Children with neurodiversities such as autism are more likely to suffer poor mental health. This is due to the differences in how they interact with the world, as well as misdiagnosis and barriers to support (Mind, 2024).

It's estimated that nearly half of children in kinship care have special educational needs (Kinship's 2024 *Forgotten* report). For more information about supporting children with SEND, see chapter 11 on supporting your kinship child at school.

Trauma and attachment

Children in kinship care have often experienced trauma which can result in attachment issues. These arise when children have difficult experiences. These affect how they process emotions and their mental wellbeing.

What is trauma?

Over half of kinship carers said in Kinship's 2022 annual survey that their children had experienced abuse or neglect before coming to live with them.

You might come across references to ACEs – adverse childhood experiences. These are all types of trauma experienced in childhood. The more ACEs a child experiences, the higher the likelihood of physical and mental health problems.

Examples of trauma and adverse childhood experiences are:

- the death of a parent or close family member
- being hurt or neglected
- being involved in a bad accident

Trauma in childhood affects how children develop, especially in the first 6 years of life. It affects how they form attachments to people, so they may struggle with relationships and friendships. Trauma will affect a child's behaviour and can present in different ways. It can look different for children of different ages. It can also emerge at different stages of a child's life, especially during transitions – times when life is changing such as becoming a teenager or moving schools.

Children need warm, consistent care from a dedicated carer they can trust, and who they know will always be there for them. This is especially true when they are behaving in difficult ways. They are often more scared at their own behaviour than anyone else is.

What is attachment?

Attachment in children is how they bond with their carers and is usually related to how safe they feel.

If a child's carers aren't able to keep them safe or hurt them, children realise that usual behaviours will not keep them safe. Usual behaviours are crying, making eye contact and smiling. They will feel insecurely attached and begin to use other behaviours that are not healthy. They may cry uncontrollably to try to get somebody's attention. They could withdraw and become very quiet so that someone who hurts them might not notice them.

If these usual behaviours work and their carers respond to them positively, children feel safe. They spend their time and energy exploring and learning. They are labelled as 'being securely attached'. When securely attached children have traumatic experiences they can often cope better. This is because they know they have support and have people that want to keep them safe.

Tools and techniques

It is possible for kinship carers to form secure attachments with a child in their care, helping them to feel safe and secure. However, this may take a lot of time and effort. The responses that a child has developed over time have helped them to 'survive'. A child who has experienced trauma can learn that the world and people can be trusted and safe. You can help them to learn this by being constant, consistent and reliable. Their previous experiences can support them too, by helping them to see that being cautious is also important.

By learning and exploring some helpful tools and techniques, you can protect a child in your care from experiencing trauma to the same extent that they have previously. It is not possible to completely prevent future trauma. However, you can help them to build self-esteem and resilience.

Therapeutic parenting

Therapeutic parenting is a nurturing approach to parenting that is backed by research and evidence. It's a way of responding, rather than reacting to challenging behaviour. It teaches children how to communicate and behave. Using structure and routine can help traumatised children feel safe and secure. It helps create certainty and consistency, which allows their brains to process positive behaviours from their carers.

It's a successful approach to parenting all children, but these approaches take time with traumatised children. Below are some suggestions and examples on how to approach it.

How to use a therapeutic parenting approach:

- establish a structure for the child which might include routines and boundaries. For example, as far as possible set routines for when they'll have breakfast, lunch and dinner. You can also use visual timetables alongside this. Introduce changes to routine slowly and include them in deciding the schedules with you having the final say

- use the PACE model (explained in the next section) to build up trust and help the child feel safe

- avoid using punishments like time out as these can add to feelings of rejection

- avoid using reward charts which can set unrealistic expectations, instead create situations where the child is likely to succeed

- treat mistakes as learning opportunities and talk about them openly

- if a child's behaviour is unacceptable, explain in a calm way why - involve the child in a practical way of saying sorry such as tidying or cleaning up a mess together

If you are interested in reading more about therapeutic parenting, we have listed some books and resources at the end of this chapter. You can also visit the website for the National Association of Therapeutic Parents at **naotp.com**.

PACE

PACE is a way of thinking, feeling, communicating and behaving that aims to make the child feel safe. It is based on how parents connect with infants.

PACE focuses on the whole child, not just the behaviour. It helps children feel more secure with their adults and reflect upon themselves, their thoughts, feelings and behaviour.

PACE stands for:

P Playfulness

A Acceptance

C Curiosity

E Empathy

How to use PACE

Here's an example of a situation, and how to use **PACE** in response:

Peter has homework that he does not want to do. He is crawling under the table, drawing on his homework and cannot sit still in his chair. He says he can't do it and he hates the work, his school and you.

Playfulness: "Wow! Look at that homework! It looks like a dog has tried to have it for dinner! Do you feel OK, Peter? You seem quite upset. Let's put our heads together and see if we can figure this out together."

Acceptance: "It can be really difficult when you feel like you can't do something. It's not nice when you feel rubbish, but it's OK to feel like that. I'm sorry that you feel like you hate the work and your school."

Curiosity: "You usually enjoy doing your homework. I wonder what has changed today? Is there something else that is making this tricky? I wonder if you are feeling quite tired today. Do you think that is what's upsetting you?"

Empathy: "You seem to be really upset and frustrated right now. Is that right? I know how that feels, especially when you don't want to do something. Why don't we work through these feelings together?"

Managing anger

Anger is a normal, healthy emotion that everyone experiences throughout their life, from very early in life through to our later years.

People who experience trauma can feel powerless and vulnerable. Anger is a way that everyone uses to protect themselves and feel in control. Anger is sometimes used as a way to express other feelings that are hard to share. Because it's hard to contain it can seem aggressive, unkind and frightening.

An important step in helping children to understand and manage their own emotions is by practicing tips and skills to manage anger yourself. Then you can confidently guide children through the ups and downs of their emotions.

Notice signs of anger

Look for signs that anger is starting to build up and try to understand what is causing those feelings.

- what is happening when anger appears?
- how does it change behaviour?
- how does the body feel when anger appears? Some people describe a temperature rise, feeling hot in the head or tension building up from their tummy, chest and head

Responding to anger

Some common anger responses can present as:

- tantrums (a response to a child not getting what they want)
- meltdowns (an involuntary response to being overwhelmed)
- violence

In the moment, ensure that the child and everyone around them is safe. It is important to meet any anger response with love, compassion and calm.

Later on, when everyone is settled and calmer, try talking to the child about their feelings and reflect on what led to their behaviour. Getting to know your child and what might trigger their tantrums (if they're a younger child) or what might lead to violent outbursts is the first step in helping you both deal positively with anger in the longer term.

Getting support with anger

The Parent Talk website from Action for Children has some excellent advice on dealing with anger in children of different ages. Find them at **parents.actionforchildren.org.uk**.

More support ideas can be found at the end of the chapter and later on in this guide, in chapter 15.

Managing anxiety

Mental health problems are common in children and young people. In Kinship's *Forgotten* report (2024), more than half of kinship carers said their kinship children had mental health difficulties.

By understanding anxiety better, you can help your child to understand and manage their emotions and responses. Anxiety is a normal response to threat or danger and it is meant to protect us. In some situations, it helps us be cautious and avoid threats to our safety. But having too much anxiety can cause issues. It can have physical and behavioural symptoms that are unpleasant and hard to manage.

Notice signs of anxiety

It may not always be easy to recognise anxiety in a child or young person. Children will often show their anxiety in different ways. They might:

- complain of tummy aches
- need extra cuddles and reassurance
- have trouble going to sleep
- lose their appetite
- become fidgety and find it hard to settle

Anxiety in children tends to be more present around nighttime, changes, transitions, and separation from those they love or trust, such as their carers. It can also appear around stressful times like exams.

In older children, anxiety can appear as anger and aggression, risky behaviours, or self-harm. These responses can happen when children find it difficult to name their feelings. They may also have had unhelpful behaviours modelled to them by the adults in their lives.

Anxiety is higher in people with autism, ADHD, and dyslexia.

Responding to anxiety

Some of the behaviours related to anxiety can be challenging. If a child is anxious, they need a loving response with tools and techniques to help them.

'Difficult' behaviour is often due to underlying feelings of fear, insecurity and not feeling safe. Talking to children about anxiety can help them understand what is going on in their bodies. We can help children to recognise the signs of anxiety so that they can tell when they are feeling anxious and can ask for help.

There are different exercises and skills that can support you and your child to better manage anxiety. You could try:

- talking about feelings and emotions
- breathing exercises such as finger, star and box breathing
- visualising a safe, happy place

- keeping a worry book – a process of writing down or drawing worries
- staying active – exercise can reduce stress hormones
- minimising upsetting content in violent or scary TV shows, films and games
- creating a calm box – a personalised collection of things (like photographs or soft toys) that the child can go to for comfort

For more details on these techniques, the Kinship webpage on anxiety has further information and resources as well as links to videos on the different breathing techniques.

Explore these ideas with the child in your care. It might be helpful to make a list of your favourites and hang it up where you can all see it.

Looking after yourself

Dealing with your child's big emotions and behaviours can be triggering for you too, and it's important to recognise this and look after yourself. It's likely some of these tools and the style of parenting will be unfamiliar to you but this does not mean you are a bad parent or carer.

Seeking support for yourself will put you in a better position to look after those in your care. For more information about practical and emotional support see chapter 8 on becoming a kinship carer.

Getting further help and support

Reaching out for support, gaining information, and talking with others are helpful ways of coping with difficult emotions and behaviour.

If your own or a child's anger or anxiety is leading to behaviour that is difficult to manage, including causing harm to self or others, it is important to seek professional support to help keep everyone safe.

If anyone is at immediate risk of harm, phone 999 for urgent help.

Adoption and special guardianship support fund

Some kinship carers can get financial support from the adoption and special guardianship support fund (ASGSF). This is open to kinship families where the child is previously looked-after and cared for under a special guardianship or child arrangements order.

Ask children's services for an assessment, as they need to apply for the fund. The fund can help you pay for essential therapeutic services, such as creative therapies, life story work, family therapy and therapeutic short breaks. See chapter 12 for more information about eligibility for this fund.

Therapeutic support from your local authority or school

Check with your social worker or family support worker, if you have either, about what your local authority can offer your child. Local authorities have a statutory duty to offer therapeutic support for children under special guardianship orders. This can be detailed in your support plan. How they deliver that will vary depending on who your local authority is.

Some schools have counselling services in-house and information can usually be found on school websites or by asking the school directly.

NHS and CAMHS/CYPMHS support

The Children and Adolescent Mental Health Service (CAMHS) or the Children and Young Persons Mental Health Service (CYPMHS) is an NHS service that works through local teams. They will assess and treat mental health conditions. Children and young people in kinship care can be referred by people such as their carer, a GP, teacher or social worker. For more information go to **nhs.uk/mental-health/children-and-young-adults**.

If you think your child has additional needs, specialist support is available. For instance, if you think they need a diagnosis of autism. A GP, social worker, family support worker or a member of staff at your child's school are good places to seek further support. Find out more about support available through your child's school in chapter 11, supporting your kinship child at school.

Kinship support

Kinship provides a range of support services including our website, peer support services, our advice line and our programme of training and workshops. You can find a full list of Kinship's services and a list of helpful organisations in chapter 15.

Contact Kinship's advice line

You can call us for free on **0300 123 7015**

For more information, including our opening hours visit **kinship.org.uk/advice-line**

Other organisations

To talk to someone about how anger or anxiety is affecting a child or family member, some good options for support include:

- YoungMinds Parents Helpline – 0808 802 5544
- NSPCC helpline – 0808 800 5000
- Shout — free, confidential text message service. To start a conversation, text 'Shout' to 85258

Children and young people can contact Childline for free via phone, email or online chat to talk about any difficulties they might be having.

Parent Talk from Action for Children offers advice articles on a range of parenting topics and 'chat with an advisor' services.

Place2Be provide mental health support for parents and carers to help them support their child or young person's wellbeing.

Youth groups in your area may offer support and advice for young people. You can search online or on social media, ask your child's school or check with your local authority.

For contact details of the organisations mentioned above and more see chapter 15.

Books and other resources

For more information about the topics discussed in this chapter, you might find these other resources helpful:

Books

- *Draw on your emotions* by Margot Sunderland
- *The Complete Guide to Therapeutic Parenting: A Helpful Guide to the Theory, Research and What it Means for Everyday Life* by Jane Mitchell and Sarah Naish
- *Parenting from the Inside Out* by Daniel J Siegel and Mary Hartzell
- *The Whole Brain Child* by Daniel J Siegel

Books for children

Our partners at the BookTrust have compiled a list of books for children to help them cope with important themes such as anxiety. Go to **booktrust.org.uk/kinship-care**.

Card deck activities to do with children

- *A Therapeutic Treasure Deck of Grounding, Soothing, Coping and Regulating Cards* by Dr Karen Treisman
- *The Trauma Treasure Deck: A Creative Tool for Assessments, Interventions, and Learning for Work with Adversity and Stress in Children and Adults* by Dr Karen Treisman
- *The Parenting Patchwork Treasure Deck: A Creative Tool for Assessments, Interventions, and Strengthening Relationships with Parents, Carers, and Children* by Dr Karen Treisman

10. Managing contact and family relationships

"

Contact can be difficult – the more tools in your box, the better you can make it.

Kinship carer

This chapter covers:

- the advantages of contact for children in kinship care
- how contact is arranged
- legal arrangements for contact
- contact arrangements for special guardians
- informal arrangements for contact
- appropriate types of contact
- how to meet the challenges of contact
- how to plan a contact agreement

In this chapter, we mainly refer to contact as being with the child's parents. Alongside siblings, they tend to be the main consideration of contact in legal arrangements. Challenges may also come with managing contact with wider family members, such as grandparents on the other side of the family.

Contact is the term used for when a child in kinship care spends time with their parents. It is sometimes called 'family time'.

Contact arrangements will differ depending on whether you're an informal kinship carer or have a legal order and whether there are safeguarding risks.

Contact should always be in the best interests of the individual child.

Advantages of contact with family

Family time with their parents can be a big challenge for children in kinship care and for kinship carers. There might also be other family members the child would like to see, speak to or retain connection with in some way.

Although arrangements can sometimes be challenging, family contact time can help the child to:

- retain some form of contact and connection with their parents and siblings – ongoing family relationships can be one of the best things about kinship care

- maintain a sense of identity, culture and heritage

- settle into the placement, especially if parents are generally supportive of the situation

- adjust to family life and not feel like their parents have abandoned them

- talk to their kinship carer about their situation – for more information about this see chapter 9 on emotional support for your kinship child

- feel reassured about the wellbeing of their parents

- develop an understanding of their parents and their situation

Many kinship carers find that their wider family networks are a source of real strength and support. The child may want to spend time with other family members, giving you more flexibility and creating a stronger family unit for the child.

If your relationship with the parents is strained, you could ask a family member to supervise contact arrangements. You can also ask your or the child's social worker for support with this. You do not necessarily need to be present at contact, as long as it is safe and in the best interests of the child.

Who arranges contact

Contact arrangements should always be in the best interests of the child and should be guided by their wishes.

Ideally, the arrangements need to be decided together, taking into consideration the needs of everyone involved, in the best interests of the child. But this can be difficult, especially if the children are placed with you in an emergency and if children's services are involved.

Either you, the parents or children's services may initiate making arrangements for contact, depending on your legal status and the type of kinship carer you are.

Informal contact arrangements

Informal contact arrangements are a decision made between you, the parents, or anyone else as appropriate. These should take into account the wishes of the child wherever possible. You can use the guidelines and questions in this chapter to help you put together an informal contact agreement.

If you have any problems with contact through informal kinship care you can still reach out to organisations like Kinship for advice (see chapter 15 for details).

Contact arrangements and kinship foster care

The Children Act 1989 states that there should be continued contact between the child and their parents while the child is looked after by the local authority: as long as it is in the best interests of the child. Contact with the child's parents should be part of the discussion during the creation of the child's care plan (see chapter 4 kinship foster care). You can use the guidelines and questions in this chapter to help inform that discussion.

There are government guidelines on contact for local authorities in caring for looked-after children. They state that the wishes of the child should be heard, and children should be helped to communicate their wishes where possible.

Contact arrangements and child arrangements orders

If your child arrangements order specifies who the child should spend time with (this was previously called a contact order), then, legally, you need to comply with this.

You might be in breach of the order if you change contact arrangements, if this is the case speak with a solicitor. For advice on finding a solicitor, see chapter 14.

You can stop the arrangement if it poses a risk to the child (even if this breaches the order). You must let children's services and the court know if you change the arrangement in this case. You might be worried about parents taking you back to court to have the original contact arrangement enforced. The court may not make an enforcement order if it is satisfied that the person had a reasonable excuse for not continuing with original arrangement. Always seek legal advice if you are unsure.

Contact arrangements and special guardianship

As part of the assessment to become a special guardian, children's services will create a support plan with your input.

The contact arrangement will be part of this and should also detail how you can access support with contact if you need it in the future. These will be guidelines on how contact arrangements should go.

Special guardians have overriding parental responsibility to ensure that the child is kept safe and feels secure when they are having contact visits with other people in the family. For example, special guardians are entitled to refuse a scheduled contact with a parent who is under the influence of drugs or where their mental health is negatively impacting on their behaviour.

Once a special guardianship order is made, special guardians are given the trust by the court to manage the contact arrangements. It is the responsibility of special guardians to monitor, agree and adapt the contact arrangements to make sure they are in the child's best interests. You do not need to inform anyone of a change to your arrangements. However, children's services might be reviewing your arrangements and ask how things are going.

If you need support with contact arrangements, you can get back in touch with children's services to ask for support. The government's Special Guardianship Regulations 2005 set out what support services local authorities can provide for special guardians. This covers assistance for contact, including mediation services for arranging contact between a child and their parent or relative. It can also include anyone else who the child has a relationship with, if the local authority agree is beneficial to the child's welfare.

Legal arrangements for contact

Contact arrangements are clearly outlined for some special guardians as part of the court order, while others are expected to make informal arrangements themselves. If you've been involved in legal proceedings, it's advisable to talk with your solicitor about whether contact arrangements have to be followed legally (because they are a court order) or they can be adapted to suit the child as circumstances change (because they were a court direction).

Court directions advise the parties to follow the support/contact plan.

Court orders are prescriptive, giving exact details of how contact should take place e.g. frequency, level of supervision.

See chapter 14 for further information on the legal process.

Jenna, Mike, Riley and Dylan

Jenna and Mike are looking after their nephews, Riley, 9 and Dylan, 12. The boys were quickly placed with them by children's services after their mum, a single parent, was struggling with addiction. Jenna and Mike thought they would just be looking after the boys temporarily while their mum got better and because of this they felt they should have an 'open door' policy to family – letting close and extended family visit the boys whenever they wanted.

However, they soon realised that this arrangement was having a negative effect on the boys. Unplanned visits at the home where they were trying to settle was causing upset when they needed calm.

Jenna and Mike spoke with their social worker who advised them to create more formal arrangements for contact that didn't take place at their home. Although this was met with some resistance from family members, Jenna and Mike now have more control over how visits happen and how it affects the boys. Their house is now a safe haven for Riley and Dylan.

Making contact work

Guidelines for contact

Planning and organising contact time can reduce the stress and make it a positive experience for, and in the best interests of the child. You might find these guidelines helpful:

- be clear on the purpose of contact

- contact needs to be managed so it becomes a constructive and integral part of life – this needs to be a shared responsibility between carers and the adult who is having contact

- contact should be age appropriate (see information below in 'contact appropriate for the child's age and stage of development')

- it needs to be reviewed regularly

- ask for support from a social worker or an independent organisation (see chapter 15, helpful organisations) with the needs of children, parents, family members and carers when planning contact

Other things you might want to consider are:

- keeping a contact diary to record what happens at contact – this will help you review the arrangements, spot any patterns or points of concern, and is also evidence if you need to approach children's services and/or the courts to intervene

- organising and talking to your child about contact with siblings

- the quality of contact has been shown by research to be more important than quantity

- make sure you know where to get help with contact if you need it – this might mean calling the police in an emergency, or speaking to a social worker if you are worried about things

- make sure family time fits in with the child's, yours and the parent's lifestyles – if things like the venue, frequency and day of family time is not right it can add to the stress

- if there is a family time order in place from the court, always follow it unless it puts the child at risk or it becomes inappropriate for the child's age and stage of development – if this happens, speak to a social worker or solicitor

- explore ways to share information about parents and other family members even when there's little to no contact (for further information about life story work, see chapter 9 on emotional support for your kinship child)

Creating an agreement with the parents can help set boundaries and create a shared understanding. Include what behaviour is OK and what will happen if things go wrong.

You can find a checklist to help you create a contact agreement on the next page.

Contact appropriate for the child's age and stage of development

A child's needs will develop over time and so contact arrangements need to be reviewed and adapted. A baby or young child will need safe, predictable routines. An older child or teenager will need encouragement, boundaries and responsibility.

Contact might be meeting face to face, or communicating by text, via social media or online gaming. For older children and teenagers, these are methods of communication over which they have more control. But this also means that it might be harder for you to oversee and manage. For guidance on managing a child's digital life, see the digital section in chapter 15, helpful organisations.

As a teenager, it might become appropriate and safe for them to have contact unsupervised. They might also be contacting parents without you knowing about it. Having frank, open conversations together about any risks involved can help you and the child manage this.

Connection can also be keeping pictures of family or talking about family members, memories and traditions. Awareness of how trauma and attachment might be affecting your child is important for managing contact. It's crucial that the child is able to form an attachment with you as their primary carer. Any contact arrangements should not be detrimental to this.

For further advice around trauma and attachment as well as helping children to understand their situation see chapter 9 on emotional support for your kinship child.

How to put together a contact agreement

Planning your contact agreement

Before you create an agreement, consider the child's wishes and feelings, and what you will be able to manage. If contact is being arranged by children's services, this list will help you constructively input into the conversation.

Think about the questions below:

1. Who does the child want in their life?
2. What are the current arrangements? Who does the child see, who don't they see?
3. When do the child's hobbies, activities and clubs take place (so you can plan contact around the things that are important to them)?
4. Do the current arrangements need to change and why?
5. As arrangements need to be purposeful, managed, age-appropriate, reviewed and supported, what kind of arrangements are 'reasonable'?
6. What is the ideal contact plan? There is likely to be some variation, where is there room for compromise?
7. If arrangements need to change, what steps do you need to take to make those changes?
8. What boundaries might you need to set with parents and family?
9. What expectations does everyone have around contact?

10. How might the arrangements need to change to meet the needs of your child as they grow older?

11. What is a reasonable timescale for reviewing the arrangements?

Writing your contact agreement

If you are a special guardian, recommendations for contact will be part of your support plan.

If you have a child arrangements order, contact might be part of a court order.

If you are creating your own contact agreement, it can be written in any way that works for you, the child and the child's parents or wider family. It could be a written, signed document or an email.

At the beginning, it is often easier to arrange less contact to reduce everyone's expectations. If contact goes well, you can always increase the frequency.

Below are some areas you might want to cover in your agreement.

Frequency:

● weekly or monthly

● length of meeting

● if there is flexibility for the child's wishes, how will they be managed?

● when the child gets older or their lifestyle changes, how will this be reviewed?

Travel:

● how will everyone travel to the venue?

● is there any support for travel costs if children's services are involved? (this might also affect how frequently contact can happen)

Type of contact:

● there are various options, for example face-to-face, video calls, letters, online gaming, texting

Venue:

● consider safety, and whether it should be private or public

● think about comfort and accessibility

● it may be best if it does not take place at your home – a contact centre may be most appropriate – see **naccc.org.uk** to find your nearest local centre

● safeguarding – make a plan for if it feels unsafe – for example, if a parent arrives intoxicated, is threatening or arrives with another person

● special occasions – are there specific arrangements for events like birthdays?

● presents or food – what and how much is appropriate?

As well as your immediate response if there's a safeguarding issue, consider what to do if:

- inappropriate words are used
- conversations are unsafe or upsetting
- the parent does not turn up

This could include having a conversation with your child, seeking advice and keeping a log in your contact diary to discuss with a social worker.

Dealing with the challenges of contact with family

Managing contact can be one of the biggest challenges in raising kinship children.

In Kinship's *Growing up in Kinship Care* (2017) report, carers advised they had serious concerns about the harmful effects of maternal (54%) or paternal (56%) contact. Concerns included parents who were unreliable at keeping in touch, frequently let young people down or who had lifestyles that exposed young people to inappropriate or risky situations.

You are not alone if you are having difficulties with contact. We've outlined some of the challenges you might be experiencing and how you can get support below.

For children

Challenges might include:

- sometimes the child themselves does not want contact
- children can become overwhelmed or confused and as a result their behaviour can be difficult to manage before or after contact
- children can be disappointed if sometimes the parents are not reliable and miss family time
- the children may not understand why they are unable to live with their parents and can get caught up in the middle of difficult relationships between the adults
- sometimes carers need to protect the child from confusing messages and potential harm by parents

What you can do

You can:

- talk to the child – read through chapter 9 on emotional support for your kinship child for ways in which to talk to children about what is happening
- if you're a special guardian, informal kinship carer or private foster carer, talk with the people the child is having contact with to discuss changing the arrangements to better suit everyone
- if you're a kinship foster carer, speak with your social worker about what is happening and how to better support the children by making changes to the arrangements

- if you have a child arrangements order that specifies contact and you might be in breach of the order if you change contact arrangements, speak with your solicitor

For family relationships

Challenges might include:

- parents may be angry about decisions that have been made about their children, and they might unfairly blame the kinship carers

- sometimes parents are preoccupied with their own issues and may need help to understand why children are unable to live with them

- relationships between family members can be tricky to navigate

- it is sometimes the case that parents of children in kinship care have separated and formed new partnerships or remarried – there may be several family units that all have a role to play in the child's life – it can be a real challenge for kinship carers to make sure that everyone remains focused on what is best for the child

What you can do

When contact and relationships are difficult, family mediation may be able to help. The goal of mediation is agreement, but it can be difficult. Find out more about mediation and how to arrange it from our list of helpful organisations in chapter 15.

For you as a kinship carer

Challenges might include:

- if a parent undermines a contact agreement it can be very difficult to manage and know what to do for the best – you might feel caught in the middle

- if a court has made an order which gives a parent contact with their child, but you disagree about the kind of contact that should take place

- time, place and location might not be working for all parties

What you can do

You can:

- talk to the child's social worker if they have one

- talk to a solicitor

- if you're a special guardian, ask children's services for support

- if you're an informal kinship carer, discuss your concerns with the parents and reach out to Kinship or other organisations for further advice

- join a Kinship peer support group. Groups often discuss contact arrangements as these are one of the biggest challenges in kinship care

Find details about peer support groups and the advice line on Kinship's website and see chapter 15 for other Kinship services.

Contact Kinship's advice line

You can call us for free on **0300 123 7015**

For more information, including our opening hours visit **kinship.org.uk/advice-line**

Financial help

Parents remain financially responsible for children, even under a special guardianship order and would be responsible for any costs relating to contact, even if this does not happen in practice.

Some local authorities may be able provide financial support to children in need under what is called 'section 17 support' to make contact easier. For example, to cover transport costs for visiting parents.

You do not need to be working with children's services to ask for this, if you can demonstrate that the child's welfare requires this support. Contact your local authority's children's services to ask for this support. You might need to be persistent in asking for this. This money is available to parents as well as carers.

Refer to benefits and financial support in chapter 12 for further information.

Find your local authority's contact details and other local information, services and support on our postcode search tool, Kinship Compass: **kinship.org.uk/in-your-area**

11. Supporting your kinship child at school

"

A massive part of kinship care is that you want your kids to be like any other kids in school; you want them to attend and do everything that other kids are doing.

Kinship carer

This chapter covers:

- how you can find a school for your child
- how to support your child moving to a new school
- what support schools should provide
- the role of the virtual school and the support it can offer
- special educational needs support
- what questions you can ask schools to get the support your child needs

Starting school: when and how

All children in England should attend primary school from the September after they turn 4, until they are 11 years old. Your local authority has a list of primary schools in your local area and their admissions criteria. Normally, you apply for a child's school place in the autumn during the year before they are due to start school through your local authority. You will find out what school place they have been placed at in April.

Children start secondary school aged 11. You apply to your local authority for a secondary school place. Applications usually open on 1 September and you usually find out in March. Admissions criteria depend on the school. The distance you live from your school of choice and if the child has a sibling who attends already, are 2 of the most important factors.

If you are looking at private schools, approach them directly. The Royal National Children's SpringBoard Foundation (RNCSF) may also be able to provide advice, support or funding. For further information, see chapter 15.

You can also choose to home-school your child. There are lots of resources to support people who educate children at home. You can start by looking at the government guidance at **gov.uk/home-education**.

Choosing a school

If you need to find a school, then choosing the right school for a child in kinship care will depend on what your child's needs are, and where you live. You can get a list of schools in your area from your local authority. Once you have a shortlist of possible schools, start your research.

Priority in school admissions

Your child will be given priority in schools' admissions criteria if:

- they are in the care of children's services
- they have been adopted from care
- and/or they left care under a special guardianship order or child arrangements order

State in your school application if this applies to your child. However, this does not guarantee they will get a place in the school you or they choose.

As much as possible the local authority must ensure the child can be placed in a school that:

- allows your child to live near their home
- does not disrupt their education (particularly at Key Stage 4, when studying for their GCSEs)

If your child does not get into the school you applied for, there is an appeals process. To find out how to do this, search the school's or your local authority's website.

Researching schools

Some useful ways you can find information about schools are:

- visit the school website (**get-information-schools.service.gov.uk**)
- attend an open day at the school or arrange to visit the school in person
- ask to meet the school's designated teacher for children in care
- talk to the virtual school headteacher in your area (local leaders responsible for overseeing the education of looked-after and previously looked-after children – see 'specialist support from the virtual school' later in this chapter)
- talk to friends and other carers
- ask for opinions of the school on local Facebook groups or forums like Mumsnet
- read the school's Ofsted report at **reports.ofsted.gov.uk**

Moving school or class

Moves between schools or classes are called transitions. Transitions may be a difficult experience for kinship children. They may have already gone through a lot of big changes and disruption in their lives.

Schools should carefully manage transitions. You can ask the school how they can support the child, taking into account their experiences and needs.

Children in kinship care may need a longer and more gradual transition than other pupils. They might need to:

- visit a new school earlier
- visit more frequently than others who may be transitioning at the same time
- meet with a supportive teacher before they start

At home, you may want to consider:

- establishing and maintaining daily routines ahead of the transition
- encouraging the child to express their feelings and concerns
- offering reassurance and positive reinforcement

Moving school closer to you

If your child moved to a new area to live with you, they may have a long way to travel to get to their old school. This can be hard for everyone to deal with. You could think about moving your child to a school closer to your home. But you need to consider if changing schools would be too much change for them right now. You will need to find a balance between what your child wants and what they need.

Moving from primary to secondary school

Moving from primary school to secondary school can be a big shift for both children and carers. In primary school, children are likely to have had one main teacher. In secondary school they will have lots of teachers. Responsibility for pastoral care may be divided across different staff. The checklist at the end of this chapter has some questions and discussions to have with the school about how best to support your child.

Moving from secondary school to college may also be a big shift. It's another opportunity to ask the right questions and ensure a good transition for your child.

Planning travel to school

Planning for your child's journey to a new school should start well before their start date. Do a trial run of the journey if possible. Some local authorities will provide support with transport to school. Ask your social worker or search on your local authority's website.

Sharing your family story at school

You can ask your child how they want to talk about their situation with their peers, particularly if they are starting at a new school. They might want to say they are living or staying with a relative.

Discussing it in advance will help your child to manage talking to other children, so they are not surprised or anxious if it comes up.

Supporting kinship children in school

If your child is having any issues at school, you're not alone. Children living in kinship care may experience different challenges at school because of their past trauma (difficult experiences they experienced or witnessed in the past). They might:

- struggle with friendships, particularly as they get older. They may isolate themselves or be more sensitive to friendship difficulties

- not engage with education and not (want to) go to school

- be sensitive to being shouted at or told off

- display behaviours that can be challenging in a school environment. For example, they may be defiant, struggle to concentrate or bully others

- have specific special educational needs that aren't being met

The school will have dedicated teachers (see section on 'designated teachers') and special educational needs staff to support children who need extra help. You might find a team in the school dedicated to pastoral care, staff who support the emotional and psychological wellbeing of children at the school.

How schools support children in kinship care

A lot of the support that schools and local authorities are obliged to provide is for looked-after or previously looked-after children: children that are or have been in the care of children's services.

If this doesn't apply to you, you should still contact the school. Schools should support the needs of all pupils, particularly those in kinship care who may have experienced past trauma and/or who have special educational needs.

The government and all schools should provide:

Designated teachers

The Department for Education specifies that schools should have a designated teacher for looked-after and previously looked-after children. It is their role and responsibility to promote the educational achievement of those children.

In larger schools, especially secondary schools, the designated teacher duties might be shared with other staff. You can ask your school which staff have this role.

Specialist support from the virtual school

Each local authority has a virtual school. It is not an actual school, but a service to promote the achievement of looked-after and previously looked-after children, as well as all children in kinship care. Every virtual school has a virtual school headteacher.

The role of the virtual school is to give information and advice to parents and schools about the needs and educational progress of children who are or have been in the care of children's services. From September 2024, kinship carers with a special guardianship or child arrangements order will also be able to get information and advice from their virtual school. As a kinship carer on one of these orders, you can go directly to the virtual school. The designated teacher may also seek the advice of the virtual school about meeting the needs of your child, with your agreement.

Find your virtual school and other local information, services and support on our postcode search tool, Kinship Compass: **kinship.org.uk/in-your-area**

If your child has a Personal Education Plan (PEP), you should find your virtual school details in the plan. Find out more about Personal Education Plans later in this chapter.

Your virtual school should be:

- raising the visibility of the needs of children in kinship care and the disadvantage they might experience
- promoting practice that encourages attendance and engagement in education
- promoting practice that improves outcomes for children in kinship care

Becky, Abigail and Omar

Abigail and Omar are kinship carers to Becky, their 13-year-old niece. Becky was previously in the care of the local authority before the couple applied for a special guardianship order to be her permanent carers. Becky has special educational needs and has also experienced trauma.

Becky has recently had repeated suspensions from school. She had been put on a reduced timetable and only attending school in the mornings, but her behaviour was escalating. Abigail and Omar were struggling and feeling the strain of juggling work and looking after Becky when she wasn't in school.

Abigail and Omar contacted their virtual school for help. The virtual school staff contacted Becky's school and checked that they were making reasonable adjustments for her. The virtual school and Becky's school decided to hold a professionals meeting that also included Abigail and Omar, and other professionals involved in supporting Becky, to make sure they were being consistent. They all agreed Becky needed some alternative provision (other activities to do outside of school) for 2 days a week to try and break the cycle of suspensions.

The virtual school staff also:

- met with the school's special educational needs coordinator (SENCo) to look at de-escalation strategies and explain how a young person's behaviour will present because of developmental trauma

- discussed strategies with school staff such as corridor passes, safe spaces and key adults to support Becky

- provided training to all school staff on trauma and attachment

The combined and co-ordinated strategy of the professionals involved in supporting Becky as well as the alternative provision helped break the cycle of suspensions, and significantly reduced them. School staff felt better equipped to understand and support Becky. Abigail and Omar felt more supported by the network and less isolated should they have further need for support in the future.

Additional funds for disadvantaged pupils

Pupil premium plus for looked-after or previously looked-after children

Pupil premium plus is special funding for schools. It is currently around £2,500 per pupil per year. It is paid to schools to promote the education of pupils who have been in the care of children's services. Though the funding is not ring-fenced for a particular pupil, it must be spent on improving educational outcomes for those children.

Contact your school about this funding. You will need to provide them with proof of your child's status, so that they can apply. This could be a photocopy of a child arrangements order or special guardianship order. You could also get a letter from the local authority, or social worker. The school will also be able to advise about any application deadlines which can vary from school to school.

When spending this funding, the school should seek out the opinion of carers on how it can best support their children in school. Schools must publish details of how they spend the money. They must show the impact that it is having for children who are or have been in the care of their local authority.

Pupil premium for children eligible for free school meals

Pupil premium is extra funding given to schools by the government to support disadvantaged pupils. It is for children who are eligible for free school meals or have been eligible in the past 6 years.

Like pupil premium plus, it is not a personal budget for individual pupils. But it should be spent in a way that benefits those pupils. The school must provide evidence of this. You should find this on their website, where a report for each school year should be available.

If your child is eligible for both pupil premium and pupil premium plus, the school will only receive pupil premium plus funding.

Early years pupil premium

Your child might be entitled to early years pupil premium plus if they:

- are under 5
- in nursery or attending a childminder
- left care through a special guardianship order or a child arrangements order.

This is paid directly to the provider. While it is not ring-fenced for particular children, it should be spent in a way that benefits children who have left care. Speak to your childcare provider about how they can apply.

Some schools will provide:

The following describes good practice but is not necessarily found in every school.

Support with behaviour

A child or young person in kinship care may have past experiences that impact their behaviour. The school should recognise this.

The school should support your child to improve their behaviour. They should consider their difficult past experiences and incorporate trauma-informed, attachment aware practices.

Where a previously looked-after child is at risk of exclusion, the designated teacher should talk to you. They can also ask the advice of the virtual school. All approaches should be tried to avoid excluding your child from school.

One person to contact

As a kinship carer, you should expect clear lines of communication with the school. This is much easier in primary schools, where a child usually has a single class teacher. In secondary school it can be harder because a child has many teachers.

To avoid confusion or duplication of information, you can ask for a single person to communicate with. This could be the designated teacher, form tutor, or a member of the pastoral team. But this won't always be possible.

It is also good practice for your child to have a trusted adult in school. This would be a member of staff they could go to if they experience any sort of difficulty.

Information on academic progress, aspirations and teaching methods

Schools should have high aspirations for children in kinship care. They should realise that all pupils can achieve their academic potential, despite suffering past traumas. They should also understand that experiencing care is not a reflection of a child's academic ability.

The school should keep you informed about the academic progress of your child. You should be made aware of your child's strengths and the areas that need more support. If you are not being kept up-to-date, or want to talk about your child's academic progress, you can contact your child's teacher or school directly and ask.

How local authorities support children in kinship care's education

The Children Act 1989 requires local authorities to promote the educational achievement of children who are looked-after. If a child is looked-after it means they are in the care of the local authority. All looked-after children should have a Personal Education Plan (or PEP). This is part of a child's care plan.

A PEP should be started by your social worker, with support of the virtual school headteacher and should be available for the first statutory review of the care plan. It should be started before the child goes into care, or within 10 working days of going into care if it was an emergency.

It should take a personalised approach to meeting the child's educational needs, and aim to raise aspirations and build life chances. It will require different professionals to work together including social workers, designated teachers, virtual school heads and other relevant professionals. The child, according to their understanding and ability, the kinship carer, and the parent(s), should also be involved in the PEP.

A PEP should:

- assess and address the specific educational needs of the child

- establish clear and achievable educational targets

- support learning by providing tailored support and resources

- monitor progress by regularly reviewing and adjusting the plan to ensure progress is being made.

You should have a copy of the latest version of the PEP. The virtual school head should make arrangements for a PEP to be reviewed each school term.

> If your child already has a PEP, you should find your virtual school details in the plan. Alternatively, find your virtual school and other local information, services andsupport on our postcode search tool, Kinship Compass: **kinship.org.uk/in-your-area**.

Read more about working with your local authority children's services in chapter 13.

Children with special educational needs and disabilities (SEND)

In Kinship's 2024 *Forgotten* report, nearly half (47%) of the children cared for by respondents were reported to have a special educational need or disability. Caring for a child with special educational needs and disabilities (SEND) is rewarding but can be challenging. This is especially true as you navigate getting the support you need.

Understanding what your family is entitled to will help you choose a school for your child.

All schools have a dedicated special educational needs coordinator (SENCo). This person is responsible for co-ordinating SEND provision at the school. If you feel the child in your care has special educational needs, it's important to speak to the school SENCo about how best to assess these needs.

You can call or email the school, ask at reception, or speak to your child's teacher if you want to discuss your child's needs. They should give you the next steps, such as a meeting with the school's SENCo.

The definition of special educational needs and disabilities

The government's SEND Code of Practice considers a child to have a special educational need or disability if they have:

- a significantly greater difficulty in learning than the majority of others of the same age

- a disability that prevents or hinders them from making use of educational facilities of a kind generally provided for others of the same age in mainstream schools or mainstream post-16 institutions

Different types of special educational needs

Special educational needs fall into 4 main categories:

1. communication and interaction, such as autism

2. cognition and learning, such as dyslexia and dyspraxia

3. social, emotional and mental health, such as ADHD, depression and anxiety

4. sensory and/or physical needs, such as visual or hearing impairment, cerebral palsy

Identifying special educational needs

The school will often identify special educational needs through assessments and classroom practice. But you can also ask to speak to the school's SENCo if you have concerns. You don't need a medical diagnosis to ask for support from the SENCo. You might seek a diagnosis later. Speak to a GP if you want support to do this.

Parent Carer Forums which operate locally can also provide support on SEND: search **nnpcf.org.uk** for more information.

Rights for children with SEND

The government's SEND Code of Practice sets out guidelines for schools and educational settings to follow to make sure children with SEND get the best outcomes from education.

The code says that:

- children should have their needs registered on a SEND register

- children with SEND should be taught alongside peers

- schools should have a SEND lead as well as a responsible governor

- staff should be trained to recognise and support SEND in order to achieve the best outcomes for children

Making adjustments in school

Schools have a duty to make reasonable adjustments so children with special educational needs can access education and other facilities or services at school.

Reasonable adjustments are positive steps or interventions which the school can put into place to help your child.

Reasonable adjustments could include:

- developing strategies with the child to enable them to self-calm, like meditation

- using speech to text technology to support writing – this could be an iPad or other tablet, microphone or a dyslexia-friendly dictionary

- routines or rewards used at home that could be effective in school

Share with the school what reasonable adjustments you think will help, and what works at home. Ask them how the adjustments are working out at school. If you have concerns about the adjustments the school is or isn't making, you can contact the virtual school.

Find your virtual school and other local information, services and support on our postcode search tool, Kinship Compass: **kinship. org.uk/in-your-area**

Individual learning plans (ILPs)

A school may create an individual learning plan (ILP). These are sometimes called personalised learning plans or individual education plans.

The plan will detail the reasonable adjustments put in place for your child to enable them to access the curriculum. This plan should describe the special educational needs of the pupil and explain how this impacts their education. It should then detail the support your child will get in accessing the school's facilities and services.

As a kinship carer, you can review the plan to make sure it meets the needs of your child as much as possible.

Getting involved in your child's support

The school should always involve you in planning support and reviewing progress. The SEND Code of Practice says that schools should meet with parents or carers at least 3 times a year.

These meetings should be longer and more detailed than most parent-teacher meetings. The meeting record and their actions should be kept by you and the school. Support and any targets set should be shared with appropriate members of staff.

Outcomes for your child should be regularly set and reviewed, as should progress towards these outcomes.

When the school reviews your child's progress, make sure yours and your child's views are taken into account.

Education, health and care plans

The school's provision may not fully address your child's needs if they are very complex. In this case, your child may be eligible for an education, health and care plan (called an EHC plan or EHCP). Talk to the school SENCo about whether your child needs to apply for an EHC plan.

EHC plans identify educational, health and social needs. It sets out the additional support to meet those needs.

Either you or the school can request an EHC plan assessment from your local authority to begin the process. An EHC plan may include financial help to pay for any adjustments or extra support your child needs at school.

Your local authority's local offer should explain the services available for children with special educational needs. Search your local authority's website for 'local offer'.

The EHC plan assessment process

To decide whether a child meets the criteria for an EHC plan, a local authority will look at what the school has already done as part of its SEND support.

They will then decide whether an EHC assessment is needed.

If they decide to carry out an assessment you may be asked for information from your child's school, nursery or childminder. They will also ask for any information you can provide about your child's needs.

If the local authority refuses your application, you have the right to appeal.

Creating an EHC plan

Your local authority will create a draft EHC plan and send you a copy.

You have at least 15 days to comment, including if you want to ask that your child goes to a special education school or specialist college.

Your local authority has 20 weeks from the date they receive the request for the assessment to give you the final EHC plan.

Other sources of help with school and education

There are other places you can seek support with your child's education, including:

- support with school anxiety and refusal: YoungMinds (**youngminds.org.uk**) has a lot of guidance

- support for children not in school – search online or through Facebook groups for local community support for children who are not in school

- contact the school's governors: these are a group of people overseeing the management of the school. They are a 'critical friend' to the school's senior leaders. Many are approachable, and you can find out how to contact them on your school's website

For a list of helpful organisations providing support relating to school and education, see chapter 15.

Checklist: questions to ask a school

Kinship carers' experiences of working with schools form the basis of these questions. All questions might not be relevant to you. But we hope this will help guide a positive conversation with the school.

General questions

- What resources, help and support do you have in school to support my child, family and myself?
- How can we work together to support my child in the best possible way?
- Are kinship children treated differently? If so, how?
- Are there any other kinship children in the school?
- What is your safeguarding policy?
- How do you work with your virtual school? What are the virtual school contact details?
- How do you support children with transitions, such as moving up to secondary school?
- Do you have wraparound childcare?

Funding

- How is pupil premium and pupil premium plus spent in the school and how will my child benefit from this? How do you involve carers in deciding how to spend this money?
- Is there any funding for clubs or after school activities we might be able to access?
- Is there any funding for trips, school uniforms or other needs that we might be able to access?

Special Educational Needs and Disabilities (SEND)

- What SEND support is available?
- Who is your SENCo?
- What percentage of children at the school have SEND?
- What's your experience of education, health and care plans (called an EHC plan or EHCP)?

Updates and communication

- Who is the designated teacher or member of staff responsible for looking after kinship children?
- How will you keep me updated on how my child is doing?
- Do you have a single point of contact for parents and carers?

- Can we identify a trusted adult within the school for my child to speak to if they have any concerns in the school day?

- My child refers to me as [insert name], how will you ensure this is respected across communications?

- This is how we describe our family set up, how will you ensure this is communicated with all relevant staff and how will it be respected in the classroom?

- How will you consider my child's feelings when talking about mum and dad in the classroom?

Your relationship and situation with the parents will determine if you want to discuss:

- special arrangements for collecting your child from school (especially for primary school)

- who is and is not allowed to collect your child

- restrictions on parents collecting your child. Consider using a password that any adult who is allowed to collect your child will give to the school staff

- a plan on what to do if the parents come to the school trying to collect your children or ask for information about them over the phone

- at secondary school, where there are fewer controls over collecting children, any issues you think may come up around contact between the parents and the school.

Mental health, trauma informed practice and additional support

- What extra support is my child entitled to? How will you assess what extra support they might need?

- What mental health, emotional wellbeing and therapies might be available through the school? For example, is there a counsellor available in school?

- What accommodations are you able to make for my child, such as more time in exams, extra learning support or one to one time with teachers?

- Have any staff been trained in trauma-informed practices? Are staff aware of the effects of early childhood trauma and able to support my child? Do you have experience of working with children with attachment issues or who have experienced trauma?

- What reasonable adjustments can you make for young people who have experienced trauma?

- Do you have a behaviour policy and if so, does this take a trauma-informed approach?

Contact details

This section is for you to complete as you gather information from your school.

Designated Teacher

Name

Email   **Phone number**

Notes

Virtual School Head

Name

Email   **Phone number**

Notes

School Governor

Name

Email   **Phone number**

Notes

SENCo

Name

Email   **Phone number**

Notes

12. Benefits and financial support

Becoming a kinship carer brings additional (often unexpected) costs. It can cause financial strain for you and your family. If you are working and caring for a young child, you may need to give up work or reduce your hours, which will mean you have less income.

This can all be stressful. It's important to ask for advice so you can understand and apply for any support and benefits you may be able to get.

This chapter covers the different types of benefits and financial support you might be able to claim, including:

- government benefits
- support for different types of kinship carers
- support for children in need
- other financial help

Government benefits

You can check if you are eligible for any of the benefits we list here by:

- searching **GOV.UK** for 'benefits'
- contacting your local Citizens Advice (**citizensadvice.org.uk**)
- using the Turn2us (**benefits-calculator.turn2us.org.uk**) benefits calculator
- using the EntitledTo (**entitledto.co.uk**) benefits calculator

Universal Credit

Universal Credit is a payment from the government to help you cover your living costs if you're of working age.

You might be eligible for Universal Credit if you are:

- out of work
- in work but on a low income
- sick
- disabled
- caring for children

Universal Credit is a single means-tested benefit that replaced 6 previous benefits:

- Child Tax Credit
- Housing Benefit
- Income Support
- income-based Jobseeker's Allowance (JSA)
- income-related Employment and Support Allowance (ESA)
- Working Tax Credit

If you receive one or more of the above benefits, you should get specialist advice before you claim Universal Credit. You could be financially worse off.

If you claim Universal Credit, you will not be able to make a re-claim for any of the benefits above.

Who can get Universal Credit

Many people of working age are eligible to claim Universal Credit if they are in work, on a low income or out of work.

You should also:

- be a resident in the UK
- be over 18 years old but under State Pension age
- have money and savings of less than £16,000

If you live with a partner, you claim Universal Credit for your household. If you or your partner are getting any benefits that Universal Credit replaces, these may stop once one of you claims Universal Credit.

Universal Credit rates

There are a number of rates you could receive, depending on your situation.

Your Universal Credit claim is calculated monthly and is known as your monthly assessment period. The amount you get may change if your circumstances change during each month – for example, how much you earn.

Allowances and amounts

You receive a standard monthly allowance for your household.

Depending on your circumstances, you could receive extra amounts if:

- you have children
- your children are disabled or severely disabled
- you are disabled or severely disabled
- you care for someone for at least 35 hours a week who receives a disability or health-related benefit

How your job could affect Universal Credit

Particular rules apply to your Universal Credit payment if you have a paid job. If your earnings vary month to month, your Universal Credit allowance and the amount you get paid could change too.

Using a benefits calculator can help you to see how your earnings could affect the benefits you receive.

Your claimant commitment

When you claim Universal Credit, you will be asked to sign a 'claimant commitment'. This is a list of things you'll do to improve your financial situation. What goes into this commitment will depend on your personal circumstances and the age of the children you are caring for as a kinship carer.

Changes to your Universal Credit claim when you become a kinship carer

If you are already claiming Universal Credit and have taken on a relative's or friend's child as a kinship carer, your claimant commitment will change. You will not have to look for work for the first 12 months, whatever the child's age.

This is not always obvious, as it is not listed on the government's Universal Credit web pages.

You can find it stated in 'Universal Credit: further information for families' on **GOV.UK** under 'Family and friends carers'.

How to apply

Find out how much you could get and how to apply for Universal Credit at gov.uk/universal-credit

Child Benefit

Child Benefit is a benefit paid by the government to help people with the cost of bringing up children. As a kinship carer, you are entitled to claim Child Benefit for the child or children you are caring for, if:

- you are responsible for them
- they live with you for most of the time

The child or children should be:

- under 16
- under 20 and in approved education or training

Only one person can get Child Benefit for a child. There's no limit on the number of children you can claim for.

Avoiding competing claims with parents

The child's parent can keep claiming Child Benefit for up to 8 weeks after their child goes to live with someone else. This is as long as the friend or relative does not make a claim. It can continue for longer if the parent makes contributions to the child's upkeep.

As a kinship carer, if you want to receive the money directly, you will have priority because the child is living with you. If there are competing claims, you may have to wait longer for a decision to be made about your claim.

You can get Child Benefit regardless of your income. However, if you or your partner individually earn more than £60,000 a year, you may have to pay extra tax which would cancel out some or all of the Child Benefit.

Claims can only be backdated for up to 3 months, so it's important to apply as soon as possible.

It can take up to 16 weeks for a new Child Benefit claim to be processed.

How to apply

Find out how to apply for Child Benefit at gov.uk/child-benefit

Pension Credit

Pension Credit is a means-tested benefit for people over State Pension age. It is an extra amount paid by the government to top up your living costs if you're on a low income. The amount you get will depend on your overall household income.

If you have a partner, you will also need to include them in your claim as both your savings and income will need to be calculated together.

Mixed aged couples

When single people reach State Pension age, they move from working age benefits to pension age benefits.

If you are in a couple, and only one of you is pension age, you are still considered a working age couple. This means mixed aged couples cannot apply for Pension Credit and will need to claim Universal Credit instead.

Pension Credit, other income, benefits and savings

When you apply for Pension Credit, your other income, benefits and savings will be considered, including:

- your State Pension
- other pensions, like work pensions or private pensions if you have them
- any earnings from employment and self-employment
- most social security benefits, for example Employment and Support Allowance (ESA) or Working Tax Credit
- savings or capital over £10,000

Child Benefit, Disability Living Allowance and Winter Fuel Allowance do not count as income.

Additional pension credit for caring for children or young people

You may be eligible for additional pension credit, called the child element, when caring for a child or young person.

See **gov.uk/pension-credit/what-youll-get** under 'If you're responsible for children or young people'.

If you're already claiming Pension Credit

If you are already receiving Pension Credit, then you do not need to make a new claim. You can contact the Pension Credit office and advise them of a change in your circumstances. For example, that you are becoming or are now a kinship carer and caring for a child. You can report a change of circumstances by calling the Pension Service helpline Telephone: 0800 731 0469.

How to apply

Find out how to apply for Pension Credit at gov.uk/pension-credit

Guardian's Allowance

If you are bringing up a child whose parents have died, you could get a Guardian's Allowance.

If both parents have died

To get Guardian's Allowance all of the following must apply:

- you're bringing up someone else's child
- the child's parents are dead (see conditions for one surviving parent below)
- you qualify for Child Benefit (see earlier in this chapter)

One of the parents must also have been either:

- born in the UK or a European Economic Area (EEA) country or Switzerland
- living in the UK since the age of 16 for at least 52 weeks in any 2-year period

If there is one surviving parent

You could still get Guardian's Allowance if there is one surviving parent, if one of the following is true:

- you do not know where the surviving parent is and you've made a reasonable effort to contact them
- the parents were divorced or their civil partnership had ended ('dissolved'), the surviving parent does not have custody and is not maintaining the child, and there is not a court order in place saying they should
- the parents were not married, the mother has died and the father is unknown
- the surviving parent will be in prison for at least 2 years from the date of death of the other parent
- the surviving parent is in a hospital by court order

How to apply

Find out how to apply for Guardians Allowance at gov.uk/guardians-allowance

Carers and children with a disability or long-term illness

If you are caring for someone with a disability or long-term illness, or disabled yourself, you can claim benefits to help.

The main benefits you can claim from the government include:

- New Style Employment and Support Allowance
- Disability Living Allowance
- Personal Independence Payment
- Carer's Allowance
- Attendance Allowance
- Universal Credit

New Style Employment and Support Allowance

You can claim New Style Employment Support Allowance (ESA) if your disability or long-term illness affects your ability to work.

It is a contributory benefit, which means you will only be able to claim it if you have paid enough National Insurance contributions.

It is not means-tested, so other income or savings do not usually affect the amount you'll get.

You may be eligible to receive Universal Credit alongside New Style ESA in some cases. This is particularly if you have additional financial needs such as housing costs or caring for children.

How to apply

Find out how to apply for New Style Employment and Support Allowance at gov.uk/guidance/new-style-employment-and-support-allowance

Disability Living Allowance

Disability Living Allowance (DLA) is a benefit paid by the government to help with extra costs of bringing up a disabled child. You can claim DLA if your child is under 16 and:

- has difficulty with their mobility
- needs more care than a non-disabled child of the same age

DLA is made up of 2 parts – a care part and a mobility part. Your child may be entitled to one or both of these parts depending on their needs. Each part has different rates of pay.

DLA is based on the needs of your child and not their condition or disability. You do not need to have a formal diagnosis to apply.

Additional criteria apply: check **GOV.UK** to see if you are eligible.

How to apply

Find out how to apply for Disability Living Allowance at gov.uk/disability-living-allowance-children

Personal Independence Payment

Personal Independence Payment (PIP) is a benefit to help with extra living costs for adults who:

- are aged 16 or over, but under State Pension age
- have a long-term physical disability or mental health condition
- have trouble with everyday tasks and mobility

PIP is made up of 2 parts – a daily living part and a mobility part. Your mobility and ability to carry out everyday tasks will affect how much you get, and whether you get one or both parts.

The Department for Work and Pensions (DWP) will assess how your condition affects you day-to-day. You do not need a formal diagnosis to apply. They decide if you qualify for PIP, which parts you're eligible for, and how much you get.

How to apply

Find out how to apply for Personal Independence Payment at gov.uk/pip

Carer's Allowance

Carer's Allowance is a government benefit you can claim if you care for someone else for 35 hours a week or more.

Caring for someone means you are providing significant and regular care to someone who needs assistance with daily living activities due to an illness or disability. Care can include tasks such as helping with personal hygiene, cooking, cleaning, managing medications, transportation, and providing emotional support.

The person you care for should be getting one of these benefits:

- Personal Independence Payment (daily living component)
- Disability Living Allowance (middle or highest care component)
- Attendance Allowance
- Constant Attendance Allowance
- Armed Forces Independence Payment

You can claim Carer's Allowance whether you are working or not. Your earnings should not be more than £151 a week (after deductions) to qualify for Carer's Allowance.

In some cases, claiming Carer's Allowance could make the person in your care worse off financially. Before making a claim, you should always check the effect it will have. See **gov.uk/carers-allowance/effect-on-other-benefits** to find out more.

You can seek specialist advice from your local Citizens Advice or use an online benefits calculator.

How to apply

Find out how to apply for Carer's Allowance at gov.uk/carers-allowance

Attendance Allowance

Attendance Allowance is a disability benefit for people over state pension age who have personal care needs. You might need support with things like getting dressed, washing, moving around the home or eating.

To claim Attendance Allowance, you should be:

- physically or mentally disabled
- State Pension age or older

You will need to show you require regular support either through the day or through the night, or all day and all night and that you have needed help with your personal care (for example, washing and dressing), or supervision to keep you safe, for at least 6 months before claiming.

Attendance Allowance is paid at 2 rates, and you can check **GOV.UK** to find out how much you could get.

How to apply

Find out how to apply for Attendance Allowance at gov.uk/attendance-allowance

Universal Credit

If you are caring for someone with a disability or long-term illness, or disabled yourself, you may be eligible for Universal Credit (more information earlier in this chapter).

How to apply

Find out how much you could get and how to apply for Universal Credit at gov.uk/universal-credit

Support for different types of kinship carers

Depending on the type of kinship carer you are, you may be entitled to additional benefits or allowance from your local authority.

It is important to understand how the different types of kinship care affect the financial support you will receive. If you are unsure, ask your social worker (if you are working with one), or speak to an organisation such as Kinship to get advice. For a list of helpful organisations, see chapter 15.

Contact Kinship's advice line

You can call us for free on **0300 123 7015**

For more information, including our opening hours visit **kinship.org.uk/advice-line**

Foster care allowance

If you are a kinship foster carer, you are entitled to a foster care allowance to help you with the costs of caring for a child.

The amount you get depends on how many children you are fostering, their age, their needs, your experience and where you live. Minimum weekly allowances are set by the government each year and vary depending on the child's age and location. The minimum allowance is updated every April. For up-to-date minimum allowances, search **GOV.UK** for 'help and support for foster parents in England'.

The foster care allowance is paid to you by your local authority's children's services. Contact them for details of what you are entitled to. You may be able to get extra help to pay for things like birthdays, holidays and religious festivals.

You will not be entitled to a foster care allowance if you are a private foster carer and you made the arrangements with the child's parents.

How to apply

For guidance on current rates, see gov.uk/support-for-foster-parents

Special guardianship allowance

If you are a special guardian, you may be able to get a special guardianship allowance from your local authority.

Special guardianship allowance is:

- discretionary, which means children's services don't have to pay it to you

- means-tested, which means if you get it and how much you get will depend on your financial situation

A social worker can assess your circumstances, decide what support you should get and review that support every year.

Children's services will use foster allowance rates as a guide when assessing your financial situation.

How to apply

Your local authority's kinship local offer will include information about special guardian allowances. Find your local authority's kinship local offer (previously family and friends care policy) and other local information, services and support on our postcode search tool, Kinship Compass: kinship.org.uk/in-your-area

Child arrangements order allowance

If you have a child arrangements order, you may be able to get an allowance from your local authority children's services.

The allowance is:

- discretionary, which means children's services don't have to pay you

- means-tested, which means if you get it and how much you get will depend on your financial situation

A social worker can assess your circumstances, decide what support you should get and review that support every year.

Children's services will use foster allowance rates as a guide when assessing your financial situation.

You are more likely to get an allowance if the child was in care of children's services before the order was made.

In reality, kinship carers with a child arrangements order rarely receive an allowance if the order was made in private proceedings.

How to apply

Your local authority's kinship local offer will include information about child arrangements order allowances. Find your local authority's kinship local offer (previously family and friends care policy) and other local information, services and support on our postcode search tool, Kinship Compass: kinship.org.uk/in-your-area

Adoption and special guardianship support fund

Some kinship carers can get financial support from the adoption and special guardianship support fund.

The fund can help you pay for essential therapeutic services, such as creative therapies or life story work.

If you have a special guardianship order or child arrangements order, your child may be eligible.

Children who are eligible include those up to and including the age of 21, (or 25 with an education, health and care plan), who:

- were in the care of children's services before a special guardianship order was made

- are under a residence order or child arrangements order and were previously looked after

- left the care of children's services under a special guardianship order that was subsequently changed to an adoption order, or vice versa

- were previously looked after but where the special guardianship order, residency or child arrangements order placement has broken down, regardless of any reconciliation plans

Contact your local authority's children's services to ask if the child you care for is eligible.

What the fund pays for

You can use financial support from the adoption and special guardianship support fund to pay for:

- creative therapies, such as art, music, drama and play therapy

- extensive therapeutic life story work to help the young person understand and cope with their past trauma and difficulties

- family therapy to build attachment and improve the relationship between you and the child you care for

- psychotherapy (or talking therapy) for your child

- sensory integration therapy or sensory attachment therapy

- therapeutic parenting training for kinship carers

- therapeutic short breaks

It can also pay for specialist assessments that lead to a therapeutic support plan for your family. The assessments are carried out by qualified clinicians and should be focused on trauma and attachment.

The fund cannot be used to assess specific conditions unless they are part of a wider specialist assessment.

How to apply

Ask children's services for an assessment. You may need to ask the adoption and permanence team, family and friends care designated officer, or a different department. If you are not sure who to ask, the social worker who helped you get the special guardianship order or child arrangements order may be able to help.

Children's services should apply to the adoption and special guardianship support fund within 3 months of assessing you.

The children's services department that placed the child with you is responsible for assessing your support needs for up to 3 years. After that, it becomes the responsibility of the children's services department where you live.

You can find more information on the ASGSF, including how much money you might be able to claim, on the Kinship website at kinship.org.uk/ASGSF

Support from local authorities

'Section 17' support

Under section 17 of the Children Act 1989, every local authority must provide a range of family support services, which includes financial support, for any child assessed as being a child in need. You can read more about this in chapter 13, working with your local authority children's services.

That means you may be able to claim one-off payments to help pay for items such as bedroom furniture and nursery costs. If you are a low-income family, you may be able to get regular payments to help pay for the cost of caring for the child.

All support from children's services is discretionary and means-tested, which means it will depend on your specific situation. A social worker from children's services will assess the child's needs and decide if they are a child in need. They will then make a decision about what support you should get or provide a clear reason why your child doesn't meet the criteria. If you are not happy with their decision, you can make a complaint.

Any financial support you receive from children's services gets reviewed every year.

How to apply

Contact your local authority children's services to ask for an assessment.

Council Tax Reduction

Local Council Tax Reduction schemes provide help for people on low incomes with their council tax bill.

Each local authority has devised their own support scheme so entitlement to support may vary depending on where you live.

How to apply

Find out how to apply at gov.uk/apply-council-tax-reduction

Other financial help

Free school meals

All children in infant classes (from Reception to Year 2) are eligible for free school meals if they're in a government funded school.

Older children are eligible if their parent or carer is in receipt of certain benefits.

The child you are raising may be entitled to free school meals if either you or their parent receives one of the following:

- Income Support
- Income-based Jobseeker's Allowance
- Income-related Employment and Support Allowance
- Pension Credit – the guarantee part
- Universal Credit – if any earnings are below a certain level
- support under Part VI of the Immigration and Asylum Act 1999
- Child Tax Credit – if you're not claiming Working Tax Credit and have an annual income of no more than £16,190
- Working Tax Credit run-on (which is paid for 4 weeks after you stop qualifying for Working Tax Credit)

The child will not usually be entitled to free school meals if you are being paid a foster care allowance for them.

In Labour's manifesto, they advised they would introduce free breakfast clubs in all primary schools in England which would be open to all students. There is currently no timeline for delivery. Some schools already offer free breakfast clubs, check with your school if they have one and for eligibility criteria.

How to apply

You can find out how to apply for free school meals by contacting your local authority or your child's school.

Help with health costs

You can get free prescriptions, dental treatment and sight tests and help towards the cost of glasses/lenses, if you or a member of your family get one of the following benefits:

- Income Support
- Income-based Jobseeker's Allowance
- Income-related Employment and Support Allowance
- Pension Credit (the guarantee part)
- Universal Credit – if any earnings are below a certain level.

- Tax credits including:
    - o Child Tax Credit only
    - o Child Tax Credit and Working Tax Credit
    - o Working Tax Credit that includes a disabled worker or severe disability element.

You may also be entitled to help with health costs if:

- you or a member of your family are an asylum seeker who gets asylum support
- you are aged 16 or 17 and you get support from a local authority after being looked after.

The NHS booklet *Help with Health Costs (HC11)* details entitlement to support with health costs.

How to apply

To apply for help you need to complete a form (HC1) which you can order online at nhsbsa.nhs.uk/nhs-help-health-costs. It is also available from benefit offices, hospitals, dentists, opticians and pharmacists.

Sure Start Maternity Grants

The Sure Start Maternity Grant is a fixed amount of £500 to help people on a low income buy clothes and equipment for a newborn baby. It does not have to be repaid.

You do not have to be the child's parent to qualify for a grant as long as you have become responsible for the child, and they are aged under 12 months.

Usually, in order to qualify, there must be no other children in your family and you must get one of these benefits:

- Income Support
- Income-based Jobseeker's Allowance
- Income-related Employment and Support Allowance
- Pension Credit
- Child Tax Credit (depending on the amount)
- Working Tax Credit that includes a disability or severe disability element
- Universal Credit

You can qualify for a payment even if a grant has already been made to the child's parent. However, you cannot get a maternity grant for a child you are fostering.

How to apply

Check if you're eligible and apply at gov.uk/sure-start-maternity-grant

Help paying for childcare

The amount of free childcare you can get depends on:

- your child's age and circumstances
- whether you're working (employed, self-employed, or a director)
- your income (and your partner's income, if you have one)
- your immigration status

From September 2025, eligible working families with a child from 9 months old up to school age are entitled to 30 hours of childcare a week.

Depending on your provider, these hours can be used over 38 weeks of the year or up to 52 weeks if you use fewer than your total hours per week.

How to apply

Search GOV.UK for 'free childcare' to find out how to apply.

Tax-Free Childcare

Tax-Free Childcare allows you to access government help with paying for childcare costs, if you meet the criteria.

You can get up to £500 every 3 months to spend on childcare with a registered provider. If the child you care for is disabled, you can get up to £1,000 every 3 months.

You can get Tax-Free Childcare as well as free funded childcare for up to 30 hours a week, provided you're eligible for both. You can use Tax-Free Childcare to pay for nurseries, childminders, nannies and wraparound care providers. Check with your childcare provider to see if they are registered for the tax-free scheme.

How to apply

Check if you're eligible and apply at gov.uk/tax-free-childcare

School clothing grants

Some local authorities will help with the cost of school clothing for pupils whose families are on a low income.

Local policies vary widely on who can get help and what items they will give help for.

To find out what the policy is in your area check with your local authority. Some school governing bodies or parents' associations also provide help with school clothing.

Local welfare assistance

Local welfare assistance schemes (sometimes called local welfare provision) can help you if you are in urgent need following an emergency or unforeseen event and have no other source of help.

You may be able to get vouchers to pay for food, fuel or clothing or bigger basic living items such as beds, cookers and fridges. You can't usually get cash.

The schemes are run by local councils and they vary. Contact your local council to find out whether there is a scheme in your area and how to apply.

Budgeting loans

If you receive means-tested benefits, you may be eligible for a budgeting loan. This is to help with essential lump sum expenses. These might be the costs of moving home, household equipment, furniture and clothing.

Budgeting loans must be paid back, but they are interest free.

Search **GOV.UK** for 'budgeting loans' to apply.

Charitable grants

Grant-giving charitable organisations often give financial help, depending on your background and circumstances.

In some cases, you can apply directly. Often a referral is needed from an advice agency or someone working with the family, such as a social worker or teacher.

Visit Turn2Us (**turn2us.org.uk**) to search for a charitable fund which meets your needs.

See chapter 15 for a list of helpful organisations, including organisations you might be able to apply to for support.

16-19 bursary fund

The bursary fund can help 16 to 19 year-olds who are in further education or training. Some vulnerable students are eligible to receive a bursary of £1,200 a year. This group includes:

- young people in care or care leavers
- people claiming Income Support or Universal Credit
- disabled young people who receive Employment Support Allowance and Disability Living Allowance or Personal Independence Payment.

Other students facing financial difficulties may be awarded a bursary at the discretion of their school, college or training provider, who decide how the scheme will operate locally.

How to apply

Check if you're eligible and apply at gov.uk/1619-bursary-fund

Child maintenance

If the child you're caring for is not looked after by the local authority, you can ask the parents to pay child maintenance.

Parents maintain financial responsibility even if their child doesn't live with them.

Contact Child Maintenance Options for information about arranging child maintenance. Visit **cmoptions.org** or phone 0800 988 0988.

13. Working with your local authority children's services

How the local authority children's services work with you and your family will depend on your kinship care arrangement.

This chapter explains:

- who children's services are and who you might work with
- what you can expect from your local authority and children's services
- how to make a complaint

Local authority children's services

A local authority is the government organisation that provides services in your local area. In some areas this might be a local council.

Children's services, sometimes still referred to as social services, are part of your local authority. If you live in an area with 2 tiers of local government (with both district councils and a county council), then it is the county council that delivers children's services.

Children's services carry out lots of different types of work with children and their families. They have a duty to make sure parents and carers have the support they need to raise their children safely. They also have a duty to investigate if a child is being harmed by someone who cares for them.

They also have to provide care for some children who do not live with their parents. These children are often referred to as looked-after children.

As a kinship carer, you might work with a social worker. A social worker is someone employed by the local authority to promote the wellbeing of vulnerable children and adults.

You might also work with a family support worker. A family support worker may be employed by the local authority or a charity. Their role is to offer practical help and emotional support to families. They can sometimes be called different things depending on the area you live in.

Find your local authority's contact details and other local information, services and support on our postcode search tool, Kinship Compass: **kinship.org.uk/in-your-area**

What you should expect from local authority children's services

How the local authority and children's services work with you and your family will depend on the circumstances in which your kinship care arrangement came about.

There are many ways in which you might begin to work with children's services. You might not always be familiar with the procedures or teams involved. We have included some key ones in a glossary in chapter 16.

It is usually recommended that families work with children's services and follow the advice they are given.

Children's services have a legal duty to make sure children are safe from harm. They also have a duty to make every effort to support children to be raised by their parents or families.

Putting the child's needs first

Every local authority and their children's services department has a duty to act in the best interest of the child.

This is protected by legal rights listed in the Children Act 1989, as well as the UN Convention on the Rights of the Child and the European Convention on Human Rights.

Children Act 1989

The Children Act 1989 is a legal framework for the child protection system in England and Wales.

All local authorities have a duty to follow the key principles in the Children Act, including:

- making the child's welfare the paramount consideration
- ensuring there is minimal delay when making decisions for children

It also states that it is the duty of every local authority to:

- safeguard and promote the welfare of children within their area who are in need
- promote the upbringing of such children by their families
- provide a range and level of services appropriate to those children's needs

The Children Act 1989 is made up of sections. You will sometimes see references to these sections such as section 17 support. It is called this because this section of the act outlines what support a local authority can provide to children. Some relevant sections of the Children Act 1989 are listed in the glossary in chapter 16. There is also more information about section 17 support further on in this chapter.

If you are concerned about how children's services are working with you and the child in your care, consider contacting Kinship or other organisations for advice and support. See chapter 15 for a list of helpful organisations.

Kinship local offer

Guidance published by the Department for Education in 2024 states that local authorities should provide visible, accessible and up-to-date information for kinship carers on the support available to them, detailed in their 'kinship local offer'. It might also be known as:

- family and friends care policy
- connected care policy
- kinship care policy

Find your local authority's kinship local offer (previously family and friends care policy) and other local information, services and support on our postcode search tool, Kinship Compass: **kinship.org.uk/in-your-area**

The policy should explain:

- some of the legal rights and responsibilities of being a kinship carer
- what support services your local authority offers and how they will assess your need for those services
- what support groups are available
- arrangements for holding family meetings
- eligibility criteria for any financial or practical help
- how people are assessed to become kinship foster carers
- how to make a complaint

Every local authority will have their own policy and will offer different levels of support to families.

As a kinship carer, it can be useful to read this policy in detail so you understand how your local authority should be supporting you.

Family group decision making

Children's services may use family group decision making meetings, such as family group conferences. They can help families to work out how to keep children in their extended families when they aren't able to live at home.

Family group decision making is often arranged by children's services or an organisation working on their behalf. They bring together the parents and wider families of children who are at risk of significant harm or may be going into care.

During the meeting, you and the rest of the family will be supported by an independent professional. Together you develop a plan that keeps the children safe and allows the adults to support each other.

Family group decision making should involve the child as well as members of the extended family and friends who can contribute to making plans for the child's future.

Children's services should include arrangements for family group decision making in their kinship local offer (previously known as a family and friends care policy).

Additional support for children

The main ways that children's services can offer support are:

- section 17 support for children in need
- early help support

If the local authority assesses that a child:

- is unlikely to achieve or maintain, or to have the opportunity of achieving or maintaining, a reasonable standard of health or development
- will have their health or development significantly impaired, or further impaired, without support
- is disabled

then the local authority has a duty to provide the necessary support under section 17 of the Children Act 1989.

The local authority can also provide support to all families who are struggling to care for their children but do not meet the threshold for section 17 support. This is usually called early help support.

Think about what you could ask for that could make a real difference. Family support services could include:

- advice and guidance
- counselling
- parenting classes
- financial assistance (but this tends to be in exceptional circumstances)

Kinship care guidance for local authorities

In 2024, the Department for Education published new guidance for local authorities on kinship care.

The guidance includes some overarching principles that outline how local authorities should work with kinship carers.

The principles state that:

- services should not be provided solely on the basis of a child's legal status, instead they should be provided based on the needs of the child or family

- no child should have to become a looked-after child for the sole purpose of financial, practical or other support

- local authorities should seek to establish supportive relationships with potential or existing kinship carers and be mindful of the emotional impact of assessments

- effective engagement with families should consider how resources within the family's wider networks have been engaged for the benefit of the child, and empower family networks to come to a decision on how this can be done

You can read these principles in more detail: search **GOV.UK** for 'Kinship care: statutory guidance for local authorities' (page 11).

Kinship Care Practice Guide

Foundations – the national What Works Centre for Children & Families – has published a Kinship Care Practice Guide to guide professionals that work with kinship families such as social workers

Key principles included in the Practice Guide are:

- support for kinship carers should take into account the specific needs and strengths of kinship carers

- one-to-one relationships and high quality casework should be at the heart of support for kinship families

- kinship families need to be made aware of the support they are entitled to, and local authorities should actively work to address barriers to accessing support

You can read more of the Practice Guide at **foundations.org.uk/practice-guides/kinship-care**

How you can use this guidance

The statutory guidance and Practice Guide may be useful in guiding conversations you have with your local authority.

"Knowing what is in guidance has helped me start discussions with children's services about practical items we needed such as furniture, reinstating the financial allowance and adapting our home. It also allowed us to get support for family time with birth parents. Often this triggered a review of our support plan, as it had changed over the years but the local authority weren't aware.

For those areas where there was disagreement, I used information in statutory guidance and guides such as this to help describe what I wanted in a complaint to the local authority and to the ombudsman. This resulted in a review of support and better outcomes."
Keith, kinship carer

If you aren't happy with how your local authority or children's services have been working with you, you can make a complaint. See details further on in this chapter.

Promoting a positive partnership with you

When you work with a social worker, they should treat you with compassion and respect. You have the right to be listened to and heard. Your views should be taken seriously and if the social workers do not agree with you, they should clearly explain why not.

You should never feel threatened by a social worker but they should explain the consequences of your decisions. This could include what will happen if you don't follow their advice.

Social workers should respond to you in a timely manner and take your concerns seriously.

They should:

- provide you with confirmation of decisions or plans in writing
- fully explain anything you aren't sure of

You can ask them to do these for you.

"Social workers have a role to play but as a kinship carer, we are the voice of that child. Don't be afraid to speak up and fight for what is right for that child."
Kinship carer

Maggie and Harry

Harry and his older brother, Tom, and sister, Sophie, left their parents when Harry was 7 years old. After a lot of involvement with children's services, and concerns about their wellbeing and safety at home, they went to live with their grandmother Maggie. She later became their special guardian. But Maggie and the children were struggling. Tom was angry with his mum, wouldn't speak to her on the phone or go to their planned monthly contact meetings. Maggie was also struggling to deal with the difficult relationship with her daughter. She felt like she was going through a bereavement.

Maggie contacted the special guardianship order support team at the local authority children's services for help. The team carried out a post-SGO assessment and recommended therapeutic life story work for the 3 children. This was funded by the adoption and special guardianship support fund (ASGSF). As well as providing 1 to 1 support for the children, Maggie also had sessions with the therapist. When things felt more settled for him, Harry made the decision to stop the sessions but asked for them to begin again when he became overwhelmed.

Maggie also attended SGO coffee mornings monthly and a 'nurturing attachments' group to support her in her role as a special guardian. A social worker checked on the family as needed, guided by Maggie's needs. The family had the same social worker and therapist throughout the process; building a trusted relationship with the family enabled Maggie and the children to ask for help when they needed it.

Based on support available from Essex County Council

Making a complaint about children's services

If you are unhappy with the way children's services are working with you, you can challenge them.

At first, you may want to discuss the issue informally either by speaking to your social worker, their manager, or writing to children's services.

If this doesn't resolve the issue, you may want to make a complaint.

You can make a complaint about:

- any decision made by, or service provided by, a child's social worker or a children's services department
- not getting the services or help you or your child needs
- being treated in a way that is unfair or disrespectful

Parents, people caring for children, family members who are involved with the child and sometimes children themselves can make a complaint.

How to make a complaint

1. **Find a copy of the local authority's complaints procedure**
    You can request this from them directly, or it may be available on their website.

2. **Find who to address your complaint to**
    This will usually be the children's services complaints team.

3. **Write your complaint**
    It's helpful to complain in writing if you can. You can ask a friend, carer, family member or an organisation like Citizens Advice to help you if you don't feel comfortable doing this yourself.

4. **Send your complaint**
    You should send your complaint to the specific address stated in the complaints procedure.

Tips for making a complaint:

- cover all the relevant points, but be as brief as you can

- stick to the facts

- try to remain polite and calm

- be specific: use the social worker or staff member's name and note the date and time of any incidents

- make sure you explain clearly what you think children's services has done wrong, how this has affected you and/or your child and what you want them to do to put things right

- keep a copy of the complaint and a note of the date you sent it

- send copies of relevant documents – but only those that will help the complaints officer understand your complaint or provide evidence to support it

- keep notes of any telephone calls about the complaint, including the name of the person you spoke to

Timing your complaint

You should make your complaint within 1 year of the action or decision you are complaining about. If it is more than 1 year, children's services should still consider your complaint if you have a good reason for not submitting your complaint earlier.

If they decide it's too late, you can complain to the Local Government Ombudsman.

The complaints process

Although each local authority has its own complaints procedure, they must all follow the same general guidelines including the 3 stages below, with set timescales for each stage.

Stages of the local authority complaints process

Stage	Dealt with by	What happens	Should be completed	If you are unhappy with the outcome
1. Local resolution	Manager of children's services (Service Manager)	The service manager will discuss the complaint with you, aiming to agree a resolution	Within 10 working days May be extended for a further 10 workings days in a complex case	Ask for your complaint to move to stage 2
2. Investigation	Investigating officer and independent person	The investigating officer will produce a written report setting out their findings The report will be passed to the adjudication officer, who decides the response	Within 25 working days Can be extended to a maximum of 65 working days in extreme circumstances	Ask for your complaint to be submitted to a review panel within 20 working days of receiving your response
3. Review panel	3 independent people	The panel will meet to consider the complaint, and you can attend The panel must provide a written report of their recommendations within 5 working days of the meeting A senior person from children's services will make the final decision about your complaint	The panel must meet within 30 working days of receiving your request You should receive a final decision from children's services within 15 days of them receiving the panel's report	See 'Who else can help'

Who else can help

Local Government and Social Care Ombudsman

If you have gone through the complaints procedure and you are unhappy with the result, or the way your complaint was dealt with, you can ask the Local Government and Social Care Ombudsman to look at your case.

The ombudsman will decide whether children's services have done something wrong which has directly affected you and caused you an injustice.

You should normally complain to the ombudsman within 12 months of the final decision.

If the ombudsman decides that children's services have done something wrong, it may recommend that action is taken to put things right.

Although the ombudsman can't make authorities do what it recommends, they will usually act on what the ombudsman says.

The ombudsman can ask children's services to:

- carry out an assessment of the child's needs

- make sure the services and support provided meet the identified needs of the child

- make changes to its procedures so that the same problem doesn't happen in the future

The Local Government Ombudsman lists recent successful complaints on their website: search **lgo.org.uk**

Your local councillor or MP

Sometimes it may help to involve your local councillor and/or MP. You could ask them to intervene even if you are still going through the complaints procedure.

In local authorities which deliver children's services, there will be a specific councillor responsible for children and families. They might be called the Lead Member for Children and Families or Cabinet Member for Children's Services. Councillors and MPs usually hold regular in-person surgeries, either at their offices or in local facilities such as libraries.

You can find who your councillors are and contact them at **gov.uk/find-your-local-councillors**

You can find out who your local MP is at **members.parliament.uk/members/commons**

You can find details of your local councillors and MP, and send them messages directly, by entering your post code at **writetothem.com**.

The High Court

If your complaint is urgent or if you have exhausted the complaints procedure, you may be able to apply for judicial review. This is when the High Court looks at the way a decision was reached to see if it was legally correct.

Judicial review is a complicated area of the law and can be very expensive. If you are considering it, you should consult a solicitor specialising in this area of law. Strict deadlines usually apply to judicial review applications, so you should get legal advice as soon as possible.

Contact details of helpful organisations

See chapter 15 for details of organisations that can help.

Checklist: questions to ask children's services

Kinship carers' experiences of working with children's services and local authorities form the basis of these questions. All questions might not be relevant to you. But we hope this will help guide conversations you might have and help you understand your rights and responsibilities.

Understanding options

- What are my options? How will the different types of kinship care impact my rights, responsibilities and the financial support I'm entitled to?

- How will you support me, my family and the child – physically, emotionally and financially? How long will this support be for? What section 17 support might we be entitled to?

  o If you have a special guardianship order, work with your social worker to put this in a support plan. The plan should cover areas like finances, parent contact, childcare, finding suitable housing, respite, therapy, bereavement counselling, and education.

- How long will the process of becoming a kinship carer take?

Support

- Who will be my main contact?

- How often will we meet?

- How will I be kept informed of any updates?

- Can I see details of your kinship local offer/family and friends care policy?'

- What courses and training are available to help me in my role now and in the future? Are these mandatory?

- What independent support is available that can support me as a kinship carer? (such as support groups)

- If issues arise for me in the future, will you support me? (such as through mental health support)

- How will you support me in staying in my job?

Funding

- Is there any financial support? If so, how much and is it means-tested? How does this change depending on the type of kinship carer I am?

- Do you offer payment towards a solicitor if I am going for a special guardianship order? Is this from a specialist in child law?

- What funding is available for therapy for the child now and/or in the future? Is it means-tested?

- Is there funding or support available for respite? Is it means-tested?

- Can you tell me how can I access funding for things such as uniform, clothes, bedroom furniture, car seats, and cots? Or if there are other ways to get these or other similar essential items?

- If I need a bigger house, are you able to help? If so, how?

Child's background and history

- Why has the child been removed from their parents?

- How has trauma affected the child so far?

- Can you support us with life story work?

For more information about emotional support for your kinship child, including life story work, see chapter 9.

Contact and parental responsibility

- What and how often are you expecting contact meet ups to happen with the parents? When will this be established? How will it be managed and by who?

- Who's responsible for supervising parental contact?

- What parental responsibility do I have?

- Who's financially responsible for the child?

For more information about contact, see chapter 10.

Other tips from kinship carers

- Get any support that is agreed put in writing: include the length of time they're committing to that support

- Do not let anyone pressure or guilt trip you into making a quick decision

Children's services: useful contacts

This section is for you to complete as you gather information from your local authority. Try to include the local authority safeguarding team details below.

Children's services

Phone number

Out of hours phone number

Email

CONTACTS

Name	Job title	Contact number and email address

How children's services have said they will work with you

What funding children's services have said they could provide

Information about contact arrangements and requirements

14. The legal process

This chapter covers:

- how to find legal advice
- how to get support with legal costs
- key terms you'll come across
- what to expect from the legal process and being in court
- what happens next

As a kinship carer it's a good idea to seek legal advice to understand what your rights are. You might go through a legal process if you choose to formalise your arrangements.

It is important to know that if children's services say it's unsafe for a child to return home, the child should be under the care of the local authority. This will significantly affect the support you'll get. Legal advice can help you navigate this.

Understand your legal options and rights early on

It's a good idea to get legal advice early on in your kinship journey.

When circumstances change, this can also be a good time to get legal advice. For example, if you are finding it difficult to make decisions without parental responsibility.

Even if everyone agrees on the best arrangement for the child, legal advice can help you determine:

- what options you have
- the advantages and disadvantages of your options
- what financial support and other support you might be entitled to with different options

Finding legal advice and support

You can get free advice and information online. There are also organisations that give free face to face or telephone advice. If you're going to court, legal aid is available in some circumstances. You can also hire a private solicitor or represent yourself.

See chapter 15, helpful organisations, for more information.

Your kinship local offer should set out the legal support that may be available to kinship carers and potential kinship carers, including the eligibility and extent of that support.

This should cover any legal support provided by the local authority, partner organisations or the voluntary sector as well as eligibility for government legal aid from the Legal Aid Agency.

Find your local authority's kinship local offer (previously family and friends care policy) and other local information, services and support on our postcode search tool, Kinship Compass: **kinship.org.uk/in-your-area**

Getting free information and advice

To advise people applying for a special guardianship order about their support plan, some local authorities will pay towards a solicitor. This is a limited, one-off payment.

Ask your local authority for further details. It is a good idea to check the level of expertise of the person advising you on this. For example, do they have a 'Children Law Accreditation'.

You may find our checklist at the end of this chapter helpful in guiding this conversation.

In chapter 15 you will find:

- a list of useful sources for legal information which you can get online, for free
- a list of organisations and law clinics who give face to face or telephone support on the law

Legal aid

Legal aid pays for legal advice, mediation and legal representation in court. It is available to some people, in some situations, who cannot afford to pay.

You can check if you can get legal aid using the government's online tool at **gov.uk/check-legal-aid**. This tool might tell you if you are eligible for Civil Legal Advice. For more information on this see **gov.uk/civil-legal-advice**.

Applications for legal aid are usually means and merits tested.

Means tested assesses your financial situation. The lower your income, the more support you will get.

Merits tested assesses the likelihood of your application being successful, how reasonable the costs of the case are, and the benefits the case will have for you and the child.

You can also ask a legal aid solicitor if you qualify for legal aid. Use the Law Society's 'find a solicitor tool'. On the search results page choose 'family – legal aid' and 'children' to refine the results. Find out more in our list of helpful organisations in chapter 15.

Finding a solicitor

You can find a private solicitor. You will need to know if they specialise in kinship care.

A good way to find a solicitor in your local area is to speak to other kinship carers who have been through the same process. You can:

- ask for recommendations at your local peer support group

- ask Kinship if they know of solicitors in your area who specialise in kinship care

- find a local solicitor online using the Law Society's 'find a solicitor' online tool

- check if you can get some free legal advice and help with legal costs

- look for a solicitor who has experience working with kinship carers as all solicitors have specialist areas of knowledge

- ask if the solicitor has a 'Children Law Accreditation', this is not vital but means they can represent children in proceedings

- refer to the list of questions to ask a prospective solicitor at the end of this chapter

Going to court is expensive if you ask a solicitor to represent you. If parents and/or the local authority oppose (contest) the application it can become more complex and expensive. For example, this might happen if you fail the assessment for special guardianship. Solicitors may charge £200 to £300 per hour and a contested application can lead to £1,000 or even £10,000 plus bills. Always make sure you get a quote from the solicitor and ask for an estimate of the likely cost.

Representing yourself

You don't have to have a solicitor. Representing yourself in court is called being a 'litigant in person'. Further information and advice about representing yourself is available from organisations such as Child Law Advice and Support Through Court (see chapter 15 for their contact details).

It is vital that you consider getting specialist legal advice before you:

- agree to a particular type of order where there are care proceedings and the plan is for you to be the carer

- agree to the proposed special guardianship support plan

Legal terms for kinship care

Most of the legal framework around kinship care is determined by the Children Act 1989. This is a piece of legislation that sets out how children should be cared for and also details what local authorities should provide. In legal documents or information from your local authority, you might find a lot of references to section numbers. These refer to parts of the Children Act 1989 legislation.

When are courts required to be involved in kinship care arrangements?

If there are care proceedings or if you make a private law application to formalise your kinship care arrangement, a judge at the family court will make the final decision. They will weigh up the pros and cons of possible arrangements for the child and then issue a final order.

A court or legal order, like child arrangements order or special guardianship order, determines who a child should live with. It might determine what contact they should have, with who, and when this should happen. Parental responsibility differs depending on which order you apply for. You can compare these in the types of kinship care table in chapter 1.

Key terms you might come across

Children Act 1989 (and its sections)	The Children Act 1989 aims to ensure that every child is kept safe and protected from harm, and their developmental needs are met. It applies in England and Wales and is the basis of law for most children's services duties and responsibilities to children and their families. It is made up of a range of sections which cover different areas.
Care order or supervision order	A child might be living with you while under the care of the local authority. The local authority can apply to a court for a care order or supervision order if they believe a child is suffering or likely to suffer significant harm. If granted, the local authority shares parental responsibility with the child's parents and the child becomes looked after by children's services. You will see this referred to as 'looked after'. Relates to part 4 of the Children Act 1989 (sections 31-40)
Looked-after child (LAC)	Anyone under age 18 who is looked after by the local authority, either because they are on a care order or they are accommodated through a voluntary agreement with their parents. Also children under an interim care order or emergency protection order.
Child in need	This is a legal definition. A child in need is a child who needs additional support from the local authority. Without this support, they are at risk of not maintaining a reasonable standard of health and development. The local authority must carry out a needs assessment. This is referred to as section 17 support.
Police protection powers and emergency protection order	When a child is at risk of imminent harm, police or children's services can intervene to safeguard a child under sections 44 and 46 of the Children Act 1989.
Child arrangements order (CAO) (see chapter 5)	A child arrangements order is a legal order made by the family court that states: • where a child will live • who a child can spend time with and for how long Child arrangements orders come under section 8 of the Children Act 1989

Specific issues order	A specific issue order is a court order that decides a particular question about a child's upbringing. For example, which school a child should go to if the people with parental responsibility cannot agree. You are legally required to attend a MIAM (Mediation Information and Assessment Meeting) before applying for a SIO via the government's C100 form (available on the GOV.UK website).
	However, you might not need to attend a mediation meeting before applying if the matter is urgent, is a child protection issue, there is evidence of domestic violence or mediation has been attempted previously.
	This relates to section 8 of the Children Act 1989.
Prohibited steps order	A prohibited steps order (PSO) is a court order that specifies particular things that someone with parental responsibility cannot legally do without another person with parental responsibility or the courts consent to safeguard the child's welfare. For example, it can prevent contact with someone who is regarded as a safeguarding risk to the child, or prevent someone with parental responsibility from relocating with the child to another country. You are legally required to attend a MIAM (Mediation Information and Assessment Meeting) before applying for a PSO via the government's C100 form (available on the GOV.UK website).
	However, you might not need to attend a mediation meeting before applying if the matter is urgent, is a child protection issue, there is evidence of domestic violence or mediation has been attempted previously.
	This relates to section 8 of the Children Act 1989.
Special guardianship order (SGO) (see chapter 6)	A special guardianship order is a legal order made by the family court. The person or people named on the special guardianship order will become the child's special guardian.
	As a special guardian, you have parental responsibility for the child until they are 18 years old. The child will live with you permanently. You will make both day-to-day decisions about their care and more important decisions about their life.
	If you are granted a special guardianship order the parent cannot subsequently challenge the order without permission of the court.
	Relates to section 14 of the Children Act 1989.
Adoption (chapter 7)	For most kinship carers, adoption is not usually the most suitable arrangement. Instead, the family court will consider special guardianship order or a child arrangements order.
	Adoption is the process where a child becomes a legal and permanent member of a new family. An adoption order ends the child's legal ties with their family and all rights and responsibilities move to the adoptive parents, who will make decisions about the child and who they have contact with.
	Adoption permanently breaks the link between the child and their parents, which can often create complex and difficult situations.
	UK legislation for adoption comes from the Adoption and Children Act 2002.
Family court in public and private law	Family courts deal with disputes to do with children. They deal with cases where the local authority has intervened to safeguard a child. This is sometimes referred to as public law. It also deals with cases where the local authority is not involved. For example, the parents have placed the child with a relative. This is sometimes referred to as private law.

The legal process

The legal process can be complex and stressful. It's natural to wonder what will happen in court, what you'll be asked, how you need to prepare, and even what to wear.

Cases will differ depending on their complexity.

Legally, if children's service are involved, care proceedings should be dealt with within 26 weeks of them starting.

Private vs. public law proceedings in the family court

If the local authority has been involved in the care of the child and they have started care proceedings, you may go through public law proceedings through the family court. Public family law cases involve things like care proceedings and child protection matters.

Local authorities may encourage you to apply for a child arrangements or special guardianship order and offer to fund you making a private application to prevent public care proceedings. However, that could affect the support they offer you and can prevent the parents from having legal representation. You should obtain specialist legal advice before doing so.

Court proceedings and kinship foster carers

In public law proceedings, a kinship foster carer will not automatically be 'a party to proceedings' (meaning, not involved in the case), as they don't have parental responsibility. Being a party to proceedings means you have a say in the court's decision and access to the relevant documentation. To become party to proceedings, as a kinship foster carer you need to apply to the court. Whether you are granted party status can depend on the specifics of the case and the court's discretion.

If the local authority is not involved, you will go through a private law proceeding. Private family law cases heard in the family court include divorce, child arrangements (custody/access), financial remedies, and adoption.

Family mediation – before going to court

Family mediation is a way of coming to agreement about arrangements outside of court. A mediator is an independent person who can help you reach agreement. There is a cost for this. Check if you can apply for the family mediation voucher scheme being run by the government.

Before applying for certain court orders, you may, and if you are in private law proceedings you will be required to attend a Mediation Information Assessment Meeting (MIAM). There is an additional cost for this, but that may be covered by legal aid.

You may not need to attend a MIAM if:

- there are child protection concerns and children's services are involved
- the case is urgent
- the case involves domestic violence
- mediation has been attempted before

If you are unsure about whether you will need to attend a MIAM, ask your solicitor.

Check if you qualify for the family mediation voucher scheme on the government's website at **gov.uk/guidance/family-mediation-voucher-scheme**.

Find a local family mediator through the Family Mediation Council's website at **familymediationcouncil.org.uk**

Pre-proceedings meeting

There might be several hearings or meetings before the date on which the order is decided by the judge. These will vary depending on your situation and the complexities of the case.

Ask your solicitor what hearings there are likely to be, whether you need to attend in person, and what you'll need to prepare and do for each one. Further information about hearings can be found on the Child Law Advice website at **childlawadvice.org.uk/information-pages/hearings-in-the-family-court**

Preparing for family court

Here are some of the things you might do to prepare for hearings at the family court.

Read all your court paperwork

A notice of the hearing should have been sent to you by the court, this is called a C6 notice. It will give you the case number, address of the court, time and estimated length of the hearing. If you haven't received a copy, you can't make the court date or feel you don't have enough time to prepare, speak to the court office.

Speak to Cafcass

Cafcass are the Children and Family Court Advisory and Support Service in England. Their role is to promote the welfare of children and families involved in court proceedings. They may contact you and the other parties a few weeks or days before the hearing to discuss any concerns you have about the child. They carry out safeguarding checks with police and children's services, and advise the court.

File a position statement

You might be asked by the court to file a position statement before the hearing. In this statement you need to give a background to the situation, what outcome you are hoping for and why. Be sure to position this in respect to the best interests of the child.

Arrange support if you're representing yourself

You may want to bring a friend with you to the hearing with you. This is referred to as a 'Mackenzie Friend' and their role is to be with you, help make notes and give you quiet advice.

Practical preparation for the day of the hearing

You might find these tips useful in helping you prepare:

- arrange childcare for when you need to be at court and plan to have some time afterwards to reflect and wind down

- find out where you need to go ahead of time and check the journey

- prepare all the paperwork you need to take with you

- ensure you arrive early – courts often require you to be there at least 30 minutes beforehand

- the court must make reasonable adjustments for accessibility - if you have a disability or need an interpreter, get in touch with the court beforehand

- there are no rules around what you should wear, but dress smartly if you can

- you might want to take refreshments and pens, pencils and notepaper

- in some courts and in certain circumstances, the hearing may take place remotely via a video link. If this is the case, check your internet connection and find a quiet place before it starts

What do I need to do when I arrive at court?

When you arrive at court, go through security and approach the usher's desk to present your court paperwork. The usher will let you know which room you will be in.

You do not need to sit with any of the other parties. If available, you can ask for a private room or space if you need it.

Once the case is ready to be heard, the case number will normally be announced over a speaker.

It is quite likely that the Cafcass officer or legal representative for the other party will try and find you before the hearing so that they can discuss a way forward.

Sometimes, issues can be resolved before you get into court, but, if not, the time may still be used productively to see if there has been any change in the parties' positions.

During the hearing

It's natural to be nervous and anxious about the process. If you're representing yourself, the judge will know, so don't be afraid to ask any questions of them or the court staff. You can ask a legal representative or the court clerk where you need to sit.

How to address the judge

There are different ways to address different judges:

- **District judges** are referred to as 'Sir' or 'Madam'
- **Magistrates** can be addressed as both 'Sir' or 'Madam' or 'Your Worships'
- **Circuit judges** may be referred to as 'Your Honour'

Ask the court usher to tell you how to address the judge if you're unsure.

Some other things you might find helpful to remember for the hearing:

- make sure that your mobile phone is switched off
- when you are asked to speak
    - do not raise your voice
    - do not interrupt
    - be courteous
    - speak slowly and clearly so that the judge can make notes
    - be truthful and to the point
    - if you do not understand a question, do not be afraid to ask them to repeat or rephrase it
- make your own notes: highlight any important dates and any court directions
- if the other party or their legal representative is speaking and you want to raise a point about it, write it down and raise it when they've finished
- during the hearing the judge will weigh up the pros and cons of all options presented to them and will make a final decision

After the hearing

These things might happen after the hearing:

- if you or the other party has a legal representative they might be asked to draft an order – this is the formal writing-up of the directions given by the judge. This might be done while you wait after the hearing or emailed to you for approval
- compare any notes you made to what was drafted, and let the legal representative know if you have any amendments or questions
- once it's approved it is sent to the judge for 'sealing'
- you might be given dates as to when certain things have to be done, and when the next hearing is, if there will be one

Family proceedings are confidential, therefore it's important not to show any evidence or court documents to anyone not involved in the proceedings.

It's natural to feel emotionally exhausted after a hearing, and you should make sure you find time for yourself and your family. This might be a good time to reach out to your local peer support group or Kinship's 'Someone Like Me' listening service for further support. See chapter 15 for more details.

Appealing a decision

A court may deny an application for a legal order if it determines that it is not needed, is not in the best interests of the child or if it thinks a different arrangement is more suitable.

You can appeal decisions made by the court, but there needs to be grounds for the appeal. You should ask for legal advice as this can be very complex. Child Law Advice's website has further information on appeals at **childlawadvice.org.uk/information-pages/appeals**

Support after your order is granted

The support you can access after your order is granted will change from your previous arrangement. It varies depending on the order. For instance, if you were previously a kinship foster carer, and are granted a special guardianship order, you will be entitled to different benefits.

It's crucial you make sure you get the support you need detailed in your special guardianship support plan.

For details about the support you can get from your local authority check the relevant chapters on the different types of kinship care. You can also read information about working with your local authority children's services in chapter 13 and benefits you might be entitled to in chapter 12.

Court orders after you become a special guardian or get a child arrangements order

Kinship carers often worry about parents challenging orders and decisions. For more information about parental responsibility with special guardianship orders and child arrangements orders, see the sections in those chapters.

You can make additional applications in relation to existing court proceedings. For example, you can also apply for a specific issues order or prohibited steps order on top of a CAO or SGO.

Varying or ending (discharging) a legal order

There might be a time when the legal order you hold no longer suits you, your kinship child or your family's situation. You can only do this through an application to court and the judge will make the final decision. As a special guardian, you are eligible to make this application.

The focus of the court's decision will be on the welfare of the child, as set out in the welfare checklist:
childlawadvice.org.uk/information-pages/the-welfare-checklist

Before going back to court to have a legal order varied or ended, it's a good idea to get legal advice.

✓ Checklist: questions to ask your solicitor

Kinship carers' experiences of working with solicitors form the basis of these questions. All questions might not be relevant to you. Its intention is to help guide conversations and support you to obtain helpful legal advice, helping you to understand your rights and responsibilities.

Questions that might help you choose the right solicitor

Look for local solicitors by asking at your local kinship peer support group, or go to the Law Society's 'Find a solicitor' online tool.

These questions are for those that are finding the right solicitor to represent you and your family. You might find it helpful to speak to several solicitors before choosing the right organisation for you.

- Do you specialise in public law or private law?

- What are your hourly costs?

- What would you estimate the total likely cost of my case to be?

- Do you offer any payment plans?

- Do you offer legal aid?

- What do you expect the timescale to be for my case?

- What experience do you have of working on kinship cases?

- Do you have a 'Children Law Accreditation'?

- How will you keep me updated through the case?

- Can you advise me on long-term support planning for the child's future, beyond getting the order, including how to get access to therapy, financial support and difficulties over contact?

Initial questions

These questions are for when you might be first considering whether kinship care is the right decision for you:

- Can you explain the different type of kinship care and how that might impact my rights, responsibilities and financial support available?

- What support can I ask for and what am I likely to get based on your experience? This might include financial, therapeutic and housing support

- How much parental responsibility will I have for the child? What parental responsibility will the parents have? Can you advise what I will and won't be able to do depending on the legal arrangement. For example: can I take the child on holiday? Who can make medical decisions?

- How long will the legal process take?

- How will my voice and the voice of the child be heard?

- I'm considering a special guardianship order. Will you be able to review my support plan and advise what else should be included?

Finances

These questions are related to financial support you might want to seek in any arrangement:

- Can you ensure non-means tested financial support is written into any agreement? And that the financial support will be in place until the child turns 18?

- Can you ensure additional financial support is provided for birthdays and holidays?

- Are there any additional legal costs that I may need to account for, both now and in the future?

Contact

- Who makes decisions about parental contact (for example, how often, when and where)?

- Do I have the right to change or refuse access based on the best interests of the child?

- What rights do the parents have? Are they able to take us back to court in the future? If they do, what happens then?

Court proceedings

- How will you keep us up to date with how things are progressing?

- What are the steps in this process?

- Will I need to attend a MIAM? (Mediation Information and Assessment Meeting)

- Who will be my main point of contact?

- Will I be involved directly in any court proceedings? What should I expect?

- Will the child/ren be involved in any court proceedings? What should we expect?

- What happens if I disagree with the outcome of the court proceedings?

15. Helpful organisations

Kinship

Kinship is the leading kinship care charity in England and Wales. We provide a range of information, advice and support for kinship carers. Find out more about how we can support you below.

Information and advice

We provide information and advice on all issues affecting kinship carers including:

- welfare benefits and other sources of financial support
- employment rights
- housing
- education
- caring for a child with special needs

You can find information and advice on our website. Find out more at **kinship.org.uk/advice**

You can also speak to a member of our advice team by calling 0300 123 7015 or visiting our website and completing our online enquiry form. The advice team are specialists in supporting kinship carers and can support you no matter where you are on your kinship journey.

Find out more at **kinship.org.uk/advice-line**

Find support in your area

You can use Kinship Compass, our postcode search tool, to find local services to support you as a kinship carer.

Enter your location or postcode to find useful support and services near you including:

- support groups
- local authority teams and contact details
- your local kinship offer or family and friends care policy
- your virtual school
- your nearest legal advice clinic

Visit **kinship.org.uk/in-your-area**

Talk to another kinship carer

We know being a kinship carer can feel lonely but speaking to others in a similar situation to you can make a big difference.

Peer support groups

Kinship, funded by the Department for Education, is supporting kinship carers to set up peer support groups in their local area or online. There are now hundreds of peer support groups across England, providing a space for kinship carers to connect.

Peer support groups are a great opportunity to speak to other kinship carers in a similar situation to you, to understand more about their experiences and hear their advice and tips. If there is no peer support group in your area, or you'd like to set one up, the Kinship team can support you.

"Before I joined the group, nobody really understood what it was like. Your friends, your family, obviously say all the right things. 'Oh, you're very brave. I couldn't do it. It must be really hard for you.' But talking to the group, we learn from each other or we can just listen and we can understand. It's a shoulder to cry on, someone to trust."
Kinship carer talking about attending a peer support group

Find out more and discover your local peer support group at **kinship.org.uk/groups**

Someone Like Me

'Someone Like Me' is a free service where you can speak to a specially trained kinship carer volunteer on the phone. They will listen, understand, and support you. You can have up to 3 phone calls with one volunteer.

Being a kinship carer can be tough, there can be moments of real joy and happiness, mixed with tough times. In the not-so-great times, speaking to someone else who has been in a similar situation can be invaluable.

"It was a pleasure to talk with 'Someone Like Me', I felt more motivated especially when I told her about going back to work. She lifted my spirits."
Kinship carer

Find out more at **kinship.org.uk/someone-like-me**

Free workshops and events

We have developed the first training and support service for kinship carers in England (funded by the Department for Education). Our free workshops and events cover a range of topics such as an introduction to kinship care, managing contact, dealing with challenging behaviour and understanding trauma. As well as an opportunity to learn, they're a great way to meet and connect with other kinship carers too.

Workshops and events take place throughout the year both online and in-person. Check our website for the latest events and updates.

"Attending the workshops gives hope in these challenging situations where you can feel very ignorant or alone. The solidarity and support of others on the Kinship journey is invaluable."
Kinship carer

Find the latest workshops and events at **kinship.org.uk/events**

Our other services

Kinship offers a range of other services that different local authorities provide to kinship carers.

These services include:

- remote one-to-one support with a specialist project worker, you might hear this called Kinship Reach

- intensive in-person one-to-one support over 6 months with a specialist project worker and support groups in the community, you might hear this called Kinship Connected

Availability depends on your local authority and a referral is normally completed by your social worker. Speak to your children's services department to see if they offer any of these services.

Join our community

Kinship is made by and for our community of kinship carers. You can be a part of that community.

To keep up to date with news and stories on kinship care and our work, sign up to receive regular email updates from the team.

Join our community at **kinship.org.uk/community**

Other helpful organisations

We know that it can feel overwhelming navigating kinship care. As well as services and support from Kinship, there are lots of other organisations who can support you with specialist information and advice.

We've gathered information about organisations that might be helpful. They are arranged by different topic areas in alphabetical order. Where a phone number is listed, it is a helpline.

Adoption	
Adoption UK Support, community and advocacy for adopted people and those parenting children who cannot live with their parents.	0300 666 0006 adoptionuk.org info@adoptionuk.org
Adoption England Working with funding from the Department for Education, they work in collaboration with regional adoption agencies to improve adoption practice and develop support and services.	adoptionengland.co.uk nationalwork@adoptionengland.co.uk

Benefits and financial support	
Benefits calculator Anonymous, free and independent benefits calculators.	gov.uk/benefits-calculators
Buttle UK A charity dedicated to helping children and young people in the UK who have experienced crisis. They offer a range of 'Chances for Children' grants.	buttleuk.org
Citizens Advice Confidential, impartial and independent advice online, over the phone and in person, for free.	0800 144 8848 citizensadvice.org.uk
EntitledTo A benefits calculator that enables you check what means-tested benefits you're entitled to.	entitledto.co.uk
Family Action Practical, emotional and financial support to those who are experiencing poverty, disadvantage and social isolation.	family-action.org.uk
Turn2us Information and practical support for people struggling with their finances. Website includes a benefits calculator, and grants search.	turn2us.org.uk

Bereavement

Grief Encounter A charity supporting bereaved children and young people through counselling, workshops, therapy and a free, confidential helpline called grief talk.	0808 802 0111 griefencounter.org.uk
Winston's Wish A childhood bereavement charity supporting children and their families after the death of someone important. They offer a free bereavement support helpline.	08088 020 021 winstonswish.org

Contact

Family Mediation Council Advice and information on family mediation and a search tool for finding a local mediator.	familymediationcouncil.org.uk
National Association of Child Contact Centres (NACCC) Charity providing safe spaces where children can meet the parents they don't live with. Search their website for your nearest local contact centre.	naccc.org.uk
Relate Counselling, support and information to help with couple and family relationships.	0300 100 1234 relate.org.uk

Debt

Debt Advice Foundation Free confidential support and advice to anyone worried about loans, credit and debt.	0800 043 40 50 debtadvicefoundation.org
National Debt Line Free, impartial, expert debt advice.	0808 808 4000 nationaldebtline.org
Step Change Expert debt help and advice and fee-free debt management.	0800 138 1111 stepchange.org

Digital safety

Childnet Information and guidance on a range of key online safety topics.	childnet.com
Internet Matters Information on internet safety, including safety settings for your child's devices and apps.	internetmatters.org
NSPCC Resources for phone safety, online safety, online toxicity, online bullying.	nspcc.org.uk
UK Safer Internet Centre Resources on internet safety for parents and carers.	saferinternet.org.uk

Domestic abuse

NSPCC Helpline A helpline to report abuse if you're worried about a child or young person.	0808 800 5000 nspcc.org.uk Call 999 if you think someone is in immediate danger
Refuge UK's largest domestic abuse organisation which provides information, a helpline and range of services for women and children.	0808 2000 247 refuge.org.uk
Rights of Women Legal advice and information with a focus on violence against women and girls.	rightsofwomen.org.uk/get-advice/family-law-information
Surviving Economic Abuse A UK charity that provides help, information and support to people who are suffering economic abuse. Economic abuse is when someone exerts control over income, spending, bank accounts, bills or borrowing.	survivingeconomicabuse.org

Fostering

The Fostering Network General information about fostering, and publications for foster carers and professionals. Benefits for members include advice and legal insurance for foster carers.	thefosteringnetwork.org.uk
Fosterline Advice and information for anyone who is interested in fostering or is already a foster carer.	0800 040 7675 fosterline.info

Housing

Citizen's Advice Confidential, impartial and independent advice online, over the phone and in person, for free.	0800 144 8848 citizensadvice.org.uk
Shelter Personalised local support, online resources, emergency helpline assistance, and free legal aid for individuals facing housing issues or homelessness.	0808 800 4444 england.shelter.org.uk/housing_advice

Kinship care

Coram BAAF Membership organisation supporting people with an interest in fostering, adoption and kinship care. Also has a wide range of publications for carers, children and professionals.	advice@corambaaf.org.uk corambaaf.org.uk
Families in Harmony Charity leading the campaign for racial justice in the children's social care sector, within kinship care.	info@familiesinharmony.co.uk familiesinharmony.org.uk
Family Rights Group Free, confidential advice to families dealing with children's services. They offer online advice, forums, a free telephone advice line and web chat service.	0808 801 0366 frg.org.uk

Legal advice

Advocate Sourcing free legal assistance through volunteer barristers.	weareadvocate.org.uk
Cafcass The Children and Family Court Advisory and Support Service. A non-departmental government body who advise family courts on the best interests of the children.	cafcass.gov.uk
Coram Children's Legal Centre (Coram Child Law Advice) Helpline for legal advice, specialist advice and information on child, family and education law, as well as online resources.	0300 330 548 childlawadvice.org.uk
Family Rights Group Free, confidential advice to families dealing with children's services.	0808 801 0366 frg.org.uk
Grandparents Legal Centre Specialist legal advice for grandparents over the phone.	0843 289 7130 grandparentslegalcentre.co.uk
Law Centres Network A network of law clinics that offer face-to-face legal advice in various areas of law. Some also have a telephone advice line.	lawcentres.org.uk/list-of-law-centres
Law Society Search for a solicitor accredited by the law society using an online search tool. Some solicitors offer a free initial consultation.	solicitors.lawsociety.org.uk
LawWorks Clinic A nationwide network providing free legal advice locally.	lawworks.org.uk
Legal Aid Agency They provide civil and criminal legal aid and advice in England and Wales to help people deal with their legal problems.	gov.uk/government/organisations/legal-aid-agency
NYAS (National Youth Advocacy Service) Legal advice and representation for children, young people and vulnerable adults.	0808 808 1001 nyas.net
Support Through Court Support for people representing themselves in court.	03000 810 006 supportthroughcourt.org

Mental health support for kinship carers

Mind Mental health information, advice and local services.	mind.org
Nip in the bud Short films that help parents, carers and professionals to identify potential mental health conditions.	nipinthebud.org.uk
Place2Be Parent and carer resources to support children's mental health and wellbeing.	place2be.org.uk
Samaritans A listening service if you're struggling with your mental health.	116 123 samaritans.org
Stop It Now Charity working to prevent child sexual abuse with information for people who have been sexually abused in the past.	0800 1000 900 stopitnow.org.uk
YoungMinds Support and help for parents and carers if young people are struggling with their mental health.	0808 802 5544 youngminds.org.uk

Mental health support for young people

Childline Support and help for young people that is free, private and confidential.	0800 1111 childline.org.uk
Children Heard and Seen Charity working to support children, young people and their families who are impacted by parental imprisonment.	info@childrenheardandseen.co.uk childrenheardandseen.co.uk
The Children's Society Specialist support for children and young people on a range of topics, including emotional health and wellbeing.	childrenssociety.org.uk
Muslim Youth Helpline Provides faith and culturally sensitive support for young Muslims.	0808 808 2008 myh.org.uk
NHS Children and adolescent mental health services (CAMHS) An NHS service delivered through local teams to assess and treat mental health conditions. Children and young people in kinship care can be referred by people such as their carer, a GP, teacher or social worker.	nhs.uk/mental-health/ children-and-young-adults/

Mental health support for young people *continued*	
SHOUT A free, confidential mental health text service for young people.	Text SHOUT to 85258 giveusashout.org
YoungMinds Support and help for young people who are struggling with their mental health.	youngminds.org.uk

Parenting	
Family Lives Help and support in all aspects of family life. As well as the helpline, it runs local services and courses on parenting issues.	0808 800 2222 familylives.org.uk
National Association of Therapeutic Parenting (NATP) Support and guidance for parents and carers on therapeutic parenting.	naotp.com
Parent Talk by Action for Children Online advice on a range of parenting topics such as feelings and behaviour, family life, school life. You can also chat online 1:1 with a parenting coach at specific times of the week.	parents.actionforchildren.org.uk

Rights	
Local Government Ombudsman A free service and its role is to investigate complaints in a fair and independent way.	0300 061 0614 lgo.org.uk

School

BookTrust A charity that aims to help children read by supporting families to start sharing stories and books together. Provides tips and advice, book recommendations and services at libraries and schools.	booktrust.org.uk
National Association of Virtual School Heads (NAVSH) An umbrella body for virtual school heads that aims to improve educational outcomes for looked-after children.	navsh.org.uk
National Numeracy Trust Provides advice, ideas and materials to help children to feel good about numbers.	nationalnumeracy.org.uk
Royal National Children's Springboard Foundation A charity that believes all children should be able to access a great education. They work with partners to identify children for whom a boarding or independent day school might provide the environment they most need.	royalspringboard.org.uk
Words for Life by the National Literacy Trust Activities and support to improve children's language, literacy and communication skills from home.	wordsforlife.org.uk

School – SEND

National Network of Parent Carer Forums The independent national network of parent carer forums for children with special educational needs.	nnpcf.org.uk
Independent Provider of Special Education Advice (IPSEA) Leading charity in SEND law in the UK. Provides information on navigating the system and securing the support your child needs.	ipsea.org.uk
Special Educational Needs Information Advice and Support (SENDIAS) Free and impartial information, advice and support for the families of children and young people with disabilities or special educational needs.	Find your local SENDIAS at Council for Disabled Children: councilfordisabledchildren.org.uk
Contact Advice, information and helpline for families with disabled children.	0808 808 3555 helpline@contact.org.uk contact.org.uk

School – speech and language	
Speech and Language UK Support for children's speech and language development.	ican.org.uk/help-for-families

Work	
Working Families Advice for parents and carers on their rights at work.	0300 012 0312 advice@workingfamilies.org.uk workingfamilies.org.uk

16. Glossary

Terms in bold are entries elsewhere in the glossary.

(1)

16-19 bursary fund

Fund for young people aged 16-19 to help towards educational costs such as travel and equipment. The fund is also available for learners 19+ with an **education, health and care (EHC) plan**. Formally under Educational Maintenance Allowance (EMA) which is no longer running in England.

(A)

Adoption and special guardianship support fund (ASGSF)

Some kinship carers can get financial support from the adoption and special guardianship support fund (ASGSF). Ask children's services for an assessment, as they need to apply for the fund. The fund can help you pay for essential therapeutic services, such as creative therapies, **life story work**, family therapy and therapeutic short breaks.

See chapter 12 for more information about eligibility for this fund.

Adverse Childhood Experiences (ACEs)

Types of trauma experienced in childhood such as the death of a parent or close family member. The more ACEs a child experiences, the higher the likelihood of physical and mental health problems.

See chapter 9 for more information about emotional support for your kinship child.

Attachment

Attachment is the emotional bond between the kinship child and their primary carer. This bond plays a crucial role in the child's social, emotional, and cognitive development, influencing their sense of security, trust, and self-esteem.

See chapter 9 for more information about emotional support for your kinship child.

(C)

Care leavers

Depending on eligibility, some children who were previously in local authority care are entitled to support until they are 21 (or 25 if in education or training). For more information see **childlawadvice.org.uk/services-for-children-leaving-care**

Care order/interim care order

A care order is given by a court. It allows a local authority to take a child into care. Under the **Children Act 1989** a local authority can apply for a care order if it believes a child is suffering or at risk of suffering significant harm. A care order lasts until the child is 18 unless it is ended before then (e.g. by a **special guardianship order**). An interim care order has a time limit (e.g. 8 weeks).

Care plan

A written plan for a child who is looked after by children's services. It will include details of where the child should live, how to meet their needs, contact arrangements. A care plan is reviewed regularly during a **looked-after child review**. For more information see chapter 4 on kinship foster care.

Care proceedings

The family court process of children's services asking to take children into care because they believe the child has or is likely to suffer significant harm.

Child and adolescent mental health services (CAMHS)

An NHS service delivered through local teams to assess and treat mental health conditions. Children and young people in kinship care can be referred by people such as their carer, a GP, teacher or social worker. For more information see **nhs.uk/mental-health/children-and-young-adults**

Child arrangements order (CAO)

A child arrangements order (CAO), is a legal order made by the family court that states where a child will live and/or who a child can spend time with and for how long. You share parental responsibility with the child's parent until they're 18 years old unless the family court states otherwise. For more information see chapter 5 on child arrangements orders.

Child in need

This is a legal definition. A child in need is a child who needs additional support from the local authority. Without this support, they are at risk of not maintaining a reasonable standard of health and development. The local authority has to carry out a needs assessment. This is referred to as **section 17 support**.

Child in need assessment

The assessment for a child in need looks at what the development needs of the child are, and how they can be supported by the parents, and what other familial or environmental factors might affect the child's development.

Child in need plan

The plan should set out what works well and what support will be provided and by who, with goals and a timeframe.

Child protection conference

A meeting with the child's parents, family members and professionals involved to discuss the child's future health, safety and development. It can also include the child if this is appropriate.

Child protection plan

This plan looks at the likelihood of harm to a child, ways to prevent harm in the short and long term, what everyone's responsibilities are and how it will be monitored and reviewed.

Children Act 1989

The **Children Act 1989** aims to ensure that every child is kept safe and protected from harm, and their developmental needs are met. It applies in England and Wales and is the basis of law for most children's services duties and responsibilities to children and their families. It is made up of a range of sections which cover different areas.

Children and young people's mental health services (CYPMHS)

A newer term for **CAMHS**.

Children's services

The part of the local authority which is responsible for social care services for children and families. You may sometimes hear children's services referred to as 'social services'. The 2 main roles of children's services are to support children and families and protect vulnerable children.

Connected care policy

Another term for **family and friends care policy**, now replaced by the **kinship local offer**.

Connected carer

Another term for **kinship carer**.

Connected person foster carer

Another term for **kinship foster carer**.

Contact

Staying in touch with family, friends and others who are important to a child, whether meeting face to face, by letters, or through social media. Also called **family time**.

Custody (in kinship care context)

In a kinship care context, custody might refer to who has **parental responsibility** for the child, and who the child lives with.

(D)

Data Protection Act 2018

The UK's implementation of **GDPR**. You can make a request from any organisation that holds personal data about you under this law. For more information see **gov.uk/data-protection**

Disclosure and Barring Service (DBS) check

This is way for children's services to check details of any spent and unspent convictions, cautions, final warnings or reprimands. There are different types of DBS checks from basic to enhanced with a check of the barred lists.

You, and any other household members over 18 (sometimes 16), would require an enhanced DBS check if you're considering becoming a special guardian, private foster carer or kinship foster carer.

They used to be called Criminal Record Bureau (CRB) checks, so you might still see them referred to as this.

(E)

Early help/early prevention

Support provided by a local authority to help families access support to meet challenges and to prevent issues from escalating.

Education, health and care plan (EHC plan or EHCP)

Your child could get an education, health and care (EHC) plan if they have complex needs or need additional help at nursery or school. An EHC plan is designed to state and support the needs of young people with disabilities up to the age of 25. In England, you, your health care provider or educational provider can request an EHC plan.

Emergency protection order (EPO)

The local authority can apply for an emergency protection order when they believe a child is at risk of harm. This order lasts for 8 days and can be extended for a further 7 days.

(F)

Family and friends care policy

The former name for the **kinship local offer**. Policy which every local authority must have, to publicise the services available to kinship carers. May also be called a **kinship care policy**.

Family and friends carer

Another term for **kinship carer**.

Family and friends foster carer

A person who looks after a child placed with them by children's services. Sometimes referred to as **kinship foster carer** or connected person foster carer. See chapter 4 for further information.

Family group conference (FGC)

A decision-making meeting of family members to help them to make plans for a child's care and protection. This is a type of **family group decision-making**. For more information see chapter 13, working with your local authority children's services.

Family group decision making

This is an umbrella term for family-led decision making forums. It's when a family network has the resources, information and appropriate environment to make a plan to respond to concerns about a child's safety or wellbeing. It may include an independent coordinator.

An example is a **family group conference**.

Family help

This is a service that will be coordinated by local authorities for families who need a higher level of support. It is mentioned in the **National Kinship Care Strategy for England** but doesn't currently exist.

This service will be for families to engage with, and will support children and families that receive **early help** support, is for children in need (including disabled children) and children in child protection.

Family time

Staying in touch with family, friends and others who are important to a child, whether meeting face to face, by letters, or through social media. Also called **contact**.

Freedom of information (FOI)

You can make a freedom of information request from some public bodies such as the government, local councils and schools. The request needs to be in writing (i.e. not by telephone). You can find out more information at **gov.uk/make-a-freedom-of-information-request**. If the information is about yourself, you will instead need to make a request under the **Data Protection Act 2018/GDPR**.

General data protection regulation (GDPR)

See **Data Protection Act 2018**

Independent reviewing officer (IRO)

The independent reviewing officer is the person who chairs the **looked-after child review** meetings and although is part of children's services, is a person independent of all the parties in the meeting.

Individual learning plan (ILP)

A document written by people involved in the education and support of the child or young person. It details how people will support and track the progress of the learner.

For more information see chapter 11 on supporting your kinship child at school.

Informal kinship carer

A close relative who is taking care of the child on behalf of their parents. The local authority has no major involvement and there is no court order in place.

Informal kinship carers can be more distant family relatives or family friends in some cases. For more information see chapter 2 on informal kinship care.

(K)

Kinship care

Kinship care is when a child lives full-time or most of the time with a relative or close family friend. This is usually because their parents are not able to care for them. This can be a temporary or permanent arrangement.

For a full government definition, see chapter 1 on what is kinship care?

Kinship care policy

Another term for **family and friends care policy**, now replaced by the **kinship local offer**.

Kinship foster carer

A person who looks after a child placed with them by children's services. Sometimes referred to as **family and friends foster carer** or connected person foster carer. See chapter 4 for further information.

Kinship local offer

Information for kinship carers on the support available to them in their area, which should be published by local authorities. Previously known as **family and friends care policy, connected care policy** or **kinship care policy**.

(L)

LAC review

See **looked-after child (LAC) review**.

Legal order

In the context of kinship care, it is a decision made by the court that determines who has responsibility for a child and who the child lives with.

Life story

Life story work is a therapeutic process aimed at helping individuals, particularly children and young people in care, to understand and make sense of their personal histories and experiences.

For more information, see chapter 9 about emotional support for your kinship child.

Local authority

Local government in England. There are 317 local authorities in England. They are known as county councils, district councils, unitary authorities, metropolitan districts or London boroughs. In some areas there are 2 local authorities: in the context of this guide we are referring to the local authority which is responsible for children's services.

Local offer

Information about the support and facilities offered by your local authority to specific children and young people. For example, the SEND local offer is for children and young people with special educational needs and disabilities. Search: 'your council name' local offer.

Looked-after child (LAC)

Anyone under 18 who has been in the care of their local authority for more than 24 hours, either because their parents have agreed or by an order of the court.

Looked-after child (LAC) review

A review of the **care plan** for children who are looked after by children's services. The LAC review is a meeting chaired by the **IRO (Independent review officer)** and is attended by the child, the child's social worker, the foster carer, the foster carer's supervising social worker and anyone with parental responsibility.

The meeting reviews the care plan, discusses progress and makes plans for the future. For more information see chapter 4 on kinship foster care.

Mediation Information and Assessment Meeting (MIAM)

This meeting is a legal requirement before submitting many applications to take a case about children or finances to court. It needs to take place with a mediator registered with the Family Mediation Council.

National Kinship Care Strategy for England

The first UK government strategy on kinship care, published in December 2023.

For more information, see chapter 1, what is kinship care?

Parent carer forums

An organised network of parents and carers of children with special educational needs and disabilities. Parent carer forums operate locally. Search online to find your nearest group.

Parental responsibility

All the rights, duties, responsibilities and powers which the law gives a parent in relation to their child. Parental responsibility can be complex in kinship care arrangements. Refer to the chapters on types of kinship care for more details.

Personal education plan (PEP)

A document written by children's services and the child's school as part of the **care plan** for a child who is **looked after**. It outlines what needs to happen to support the educational progress of the child. It is written by any professionals involved in the child's life and the parents and/or child where appropriate.

Placement plan

A document written by children's services as part of the **care plan** of a child who is **looked after**. It outlines the details of the child's placement – how it meets the child's needs, financial arrangements, contact and decision-making arrangements.

Police powers of protection

This allows the police to remove a child from an environment where they identify a child is at risk of significant harm. Police can place the child somewhere safe such as with a relative or care facility for 72 hours while an investigation takes place.

Previously looked-after children (PLAC)

Anyone under the age 18 who was previously in the care of the local authority. Children become previously looked-after when they are no longer in the care of the local authority because they are subject to a special guardianship order, child arrangements order or have been adopted.

Private foster carer

Someone who has agreed with a parent to look after their child for more than 28 days, but is not a relative of the child.

See chapter 3 on private foster care.

Prohibited steps order (PSO)

A prohibited steps order (PSO) is a court order. It specifies particular things that someone with parental responsibility cannot legally do without the consent of another person with parental responsibility or the court. For example, it can prevent contact with someone who is regarded as a safeguarding risk to the child or prevent someone with parental responsibility from relocating with the child to another country. You are legally required to attend a Mediation Information and Assessment Meeting (MIAM) before applying for a PSO via the government's C100 form (available on the **GOV.UK** website).

R

Relative

For the purposes of this guide a relative is someone who is by full blood, half blood, marriage or civil partnership the grandparent, brother, sister, uncle, aunt, or step-parent of a child (as defined by section 105 of the **Children Act 1989**).

Residence order

Court order which gives the holder parental responsibility for a child, although they share this with anyone else who has parental responsibility. Replaced by **child arrangements order.**

S

Section 17

This refers to a section of the **Children Act 1989** and relates to local authority's provision of services to **a child in need**, their families and others.

Section 20

This refers to a section of the **Children Act 1989** and relates to the local authority's duty to accommodate **a child in need** in their area.

Section 24

This refers to section 24 of the **Children Act 1989** and relates to who qualifies for assistance from the local authority.

Section 31

This refers to a section of the **Children Act 1989.** It relates to the circumstances when a court can make a **care order** or **supervision order**, allowing a child to be removed from their parents' care. This includes situations where the child is suffering or likely to suffer significant harm.

Section 37

This refers to section 37 of the **Children Act 1989**. It says that the court can tell the local authority to investigate the welfare of a child and take appropriate actions to support that child's welfare. This could be applying for a **care order** or **supervision order** or providing support to the child and family.

Section 40

This refers to section 40 of the **Children Act 1989** and relates to the court's ability to make certain orders while an appeal is being dealt with.

Section 47

This refers to a section of the **Children Act 1989** and relates to the local authority's duties to investigate and take action when a child is believed to be at risk of harm.

SEND

Special educational needs and disabilities.

SEND Code of practice: 0-25 years

Government guidance on the delivery of **SEND** services for children and young people aged 0-25 years. It covers what must legally be done without exception, and what should be followed by law unless there is good reason not to.

SENDIASS (or SENDIAS Service)

Special educational needs and disability information and advice support service. An independent and impartial service that is delivered through local groups.

Social services

Now replaced by 'children's services' and 'adult services' departments of local councils/ authorities.

Social worker

The person who works for the local authority to provide you or your kinship child support.

Special guardianship order (SGO)

Court order which gives the holder (known as the special guardian) parental responsibility which they can usually exercise without needing the agreement of anyone else who also has parental responsibility.

For more information see chapter 6 on special guardianship orders.

Specific issue order (SIO)

A specific issue order is a court order that decides a particular question about a child's upbringing. For example, which school a child should go to if the people with parental responsibility cannot agree. You are legally required to attend a Mediation Information and Assessment Meeting (MIAM) before applying for a SIO via the government's C100 form (available on the **GOV.UK** website).

Statutory guidance

Guidance given by the government to local authorities to help them follow what the law says they should do. They should follow this guidance unless there is a good reason not to.

Staying put

Under the **Children Act 1989**, an arrangement for young people to stay with their kinship foster carer past the age of 18 with the same support from children's services as they had previously received.

Strategy meeting/strategy discussion

A meeting between a social worker and other professional agencies to discuss the safeguarding of a child. Parents and kinship carers don't go to these meetings, but you might hear them referred to by social workers.

Supervising social worker

A social worker responsible for supporting a foster carer. They should work closely with the child's social worker.

Supervision order

A supervision order imposes a duty on the local authority to 'advise, assist and befriend' the child. It may require a child to live in a specified place, do certain activities and report to a particular place at a set time. Unlike a **care order**, the local authority does not have **parental responsibility**.

Support plan or post order support plan

A plan drawn up between a **special guardian** or **kinship foster carer** and the local authority at the end of the assessment process. This plan details the support required by the child and carer.

T

Testamentary guardian

Person appointed in writing (for example, in a will) by a parent or special guardian to acquire parental responsibility for their child if they should die.

Trauma

For kinship children, trauma could be threats to their physical and emotional safety, which have happened as a one off or over time. Trauma can come from being directly affected or from witnessing something happening to another person.

See chapter 9 for more information about emotional support for your kinship child.

V

Virtual school

A virtual school is a statutory service provided by the local authority for children who are **looked after**, previously looked after or who have a **social worker**. The service ensures these children are given the best education and have the best educational outcomes.

Virtual school headteacher

All local authorities are required to have a virtual school headteacher who oversees and promotes the educational outcomes of children who have a social worker. From September 2024 this includes children in kinship care.

W

Working together to safeguard children

A government report giving guidance on how agencies should help, protect and promote the welfare of children.

Notes

Notes